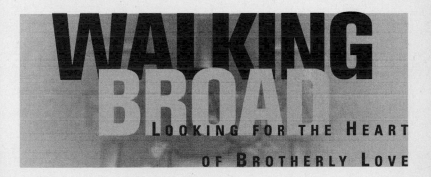

WALKING
BROAD

LOOKING FOR THE HEART
OF BROTHERLY LOVE

BRUCE BUSCHEL

SIMON & SCHUSTER

New York London Toronto Sydney

SIMON & SCHUSTER
Rockefeller Center
1230 Avenue of the Americas
New York, NY 10020

Some names and identifying characteristics have been changed.

First Simon & Schuster hardcover edition August 2007

SIMON & SCHUSTER and colophon are registered trademarks
of Simon & Schuster, Inc.

Some portions of this book were previously published in
Philadelphia magazine.

For information about special discounts for bulk purchases,
please contact Simon & Schuster Special Sales at 1-800-456-6798
or business@simonandschuster.com

Designed by Karolina Harris

Manufactured in the United States of America

10   9   8   7   6   5   4   3   2   1

"Home" by Dorothea Grossman, from *Poems from Cave 17*. Reprinted by
permission of the poet.

"Oldies But Goodies" by Grace Bauer, from *Beholding Eye,* © 2006 Custom
Words. Reprinted by permission of the publisher.

"Elegy" (excerpt) by Sonia Sanchez, from *Under a Soprano Sky,* © 1987 Africa
World Press. Reprinted by permission of the publisher.

"Onion, Fruit of Grace" by Julia Kasdorf, from *Eve's Striptease,* © 1998 University of Pittsburgh Press. Reprinted by permission of the publisher.

Library of Congress Control No.: 2007006629

ISBN-13: 978-0-7432-9284-9
ISBN-10:   0-7432-9284-7

This book is dedicated to my wife, Bettina,
who saves my life every day.

ACKNOWLEDGMENTS

A first draft of some of this book went to each of my two sons, both writers. One did some editing and e-mailed this: "Thanks for the copy. I liked it. As you can see, I have some minor suggestions. Personally, it helped clear up a few things. I always thought you fucked up my life because you were raised in an orphanage. Now I know it's because the orphanage was in Philadelphia."

My other son objected to the more self-derisive sections. "You are better than that, Pops," he said. As for a particular joke, he commented, in the lexicon of the theater, "You can't start with that—you have to earn it." I made adjustments. I hope I earned it.

I'd like to thank my sons, Marin and Noah, my brother Leonard, David Rosenthal, Flip Brophy, Max Alexander, Arline Amoroso, Grace Bauer, Stephen Berg, Jerry Blavat, Lew Blum, Robert Bryant, Paula Butler, Karen Carpenter, Fred Chase, Vijay Chintaman, Michael Coigliantry, Francis Davis, Gary Delfiner, Deborah Diamond, Grace Dith, Stephen Dobyns, Bernice Drinks, Jonathan Evans, Rita Fedalin, Ruth Fecych, Joy Fehily, Tom Ferrick Jr., Ms. Peggy Flynn, Florence Giannini, Girls' High School, Cia Glover, Paul Green, Dorothea Grossman, Alan Halpern (always), Big Jim Higgins, Ben Holmes, Leo Holt, Bob Huber, Julia Kasdorf, Gavin Kerr, Ray King, Joe Levine, Steven Levy, Tracy Lynn, Sergeant Cristifaun Moore, Willie Mosconi, Chuck Newman, Josh Olson, Peter Pagast, Carolyn Pettigrew, Larry Platt, Rock School, Michelle Rorke, Sonia Sanchez, Mike Schmidt, Molly Schoneveld, Jackie Seow, Brian Snyder, John Sterling, Hassan Stevens, Stephen Stoneburn, Street Sock Vendor, Joey Sweeney, Rocco Tarelle, Elaine Terranova, Joe Tolstoy, Anura Karthink Vivekananthan, Captain Lidia Weatherspoon, Tim Whitaker, and Harry Wiland.

Contents

WALKING BROAD

Everything stays the same is the truth of truths;
everything changes whether you believe it or not.
—STEPHEN BERG, PHILADELPHIA POET

T H E Big Red B was at least five stories high, ruby by day, aglow at night, so you could see it from miles away, like a giant firefly, right there at the very beginning of the longest straight street in the world. That's what everyone called Broad Street, the longest straight street in the world, and the Big Red B, limned in a fancy font against the Philly sky, was the sun and the moon for kiddie navigators, letting you know where you were and where you belonged. When my mother worked on Broad Street, late nights at the Cadillac Club, she told me the Big Red B stood for our family initial and I wanted to believe her so I almost did, until I replaced her fantasy with my own: it was a one-letter announcement, a red-letter celebration of the street itself, the only essential boulevard for all citizens of Philadelphia. Any move you made, or contemplated making, involved Broad Street—bus stops, restaurants, schools, pool halls, newsstands, record shops, hookers, hospitals, clothing stores, taprooms, movie theaters, or the subway that traveled beneath the concrete in a dark and parallel universe.

Broad Street was thirteen miles of enchantment that started in a quaint residential area bordering the suburbs and ran through the squalor of North Philly to City Hall and along the theaters and hotels of Center City down to Little Italy—how we salivated for the exotic food and the exotic girls with high black hair and low resistance— and then to the river where Ben Franklin used to swim after summer constitutionals. As designed by William Penn, Broad Street was 113 feet wide from start to finish, wider than any street in London. The founder envisioned gentlemanly estates and Quaker tolerance, a town leaning toward utopia. Someone should have told him: things are rarely as grand as you imagine, and never work out the way you planned.

Turns out the longest straight street in America is actually in Chicago, and the Big Red B was neither family crest nor beacon of civic pride, but a neon logo for a car dealership, Broadway Chrysler Plymouth, so named to utilize the big red B inherited from Best Market, which had been bequeathed by the Baltimore Market a generation before. Rather than the avenue of dreams, Broad Street turned out to be my road of realities: my father was pronounced dead on Broad Street; my mother was dumped on Broad Street after twenty-five years of hard labor when her photo finishing plant was sold to an international conglomerate; I flunked out of college on Broad Street, sold cameras on Broad Street, purchased drugs on Broad Street, wrote for a newspaper on Broad Street, touched JFK's left hand on Broad Street, stormed an Army tank to protest a war on Broad Street, said farewell to my first wife on Broad Street, met my second wife when she worked on Broad Street, and rode the Broad Street subway a thousand times, scared silly each and every trip.

The transformation of Broad Street from mysteriously hallowed ground to site of existential drubbing was my Philadelphia education in a nutshell: things are rarely as grand as you imagine, and nothing works out the way you planned.

1
HOME

Cheltenham Avenue to Chelten Avenue

Home
is where we
love each other
and where we
come to look things up.
Everything else
is Away.

—*Dorothea Grossman, Philadelphia poet*

LOOKING for the Big Red B at the start of the street, I find only a handwritten sign on the front door of a furniture store: WE DO NOT HAVE PUBLIC BATHROOMS. The young black salesman reiterates that policy as I enter the cavernous space. I ask him if he remembers the Big Red B in the sky. He calls for backup.

Two older gents saunter over, sipping their morning brews. I have not yanked them away from any customers, for there are no customers in this armory of a showroom; what Gordon's Furniture has in great abundance are empty seats, thousands of them, and the two senior salesmen decide to sit on a "Contemporary Living Room Group—Sofa and Loveseat, only $899—with Chaise Lounge available in 30 different colors."

I introduce myself and offer my hand.

"He wants our names now," says one salesman to the other.

"What good could that do us?" is his response.

"How could it hurt you?" I ask.

"Who knows?" says the first salesman. "If it can, it will."

The philosophy rings true. Philadelphians live by that jaundiced rule: if it can hurt, it will. It's the local version of Murphy's Law, a macabre Irish pragmatism tinged with a Jewish awareness that God possesses a perverse and ofttimes unkind sense of humor. Philadelphians have thin skin and deep insecurities; they are skeptical by nature and zetetic by training. If a team can lose, it shall. Winning is not a naturally occurring event in this town. It's not a simple matter of the glass half empty: Philadelphians question the size of the glass and the quality of the liquid—where are the bubbles, cuz?

How well Philadelphians know they reside in the former business center, former manufacturing hub, former music factory, former boxing haven, former seaport, former this, and former that. Their city is the I-95 rest stop between NYC and DC, the nation's current capitals of culture and politics, commerce and clout. Little in the last half of the last century has done anything to warm Philadelphians to the Fates, and vice versa.

You try living in a punch line without wanting to punch someone.

The two men sip their coffee in silence. More than caffeine and sugar will be needed to stir them from their lassitude. They have been selling furniture for seventy-five years between them. With some coaxing, they confess to remembering the Big Red B, and how it was removed eighteen years ago, and how nothing has gotten any better since that day of extraction, not that they blame the missing B on their chronic dyspepsia. They are openly dispirited about people shopping online, the pharmacy chain that moved next door, competitors cropping up in the neighborhood, the lack of foot traffic in their own store, the war in Iraq, global warming, the corruption in City Hall, the corruption in Congress, and, worst of all, they concur, is the goddamned economy, the shell game that feeds the rich and screws the middle class, no matter what the experts tell you.

"I work only two days a week now," says Estragon. "Just to give the old lady a break."

"He's a sweetheart, isn't he?" says Vladimir.

"It's killing me, this economy," says Estragon. "After someone pays $75,000 for a fixer-upper, who can afford to furnish it?"

"Philadelphia," laments Vladimir. "Philadelphia is down the piss-hole."

There is a long silence. Too long. I hear my heart beat. They gaze into their respective coffee cups. What do they see?

"May I use the bathroom?" I hear myself ask. The salesmen look at each other as if I have just requested their spleens.

"Only joking," I say and gesture toward the lavatory sign on the front door. They don't smile either.

This is not a good start at the start of Broad Street. Good starts are invaluable. The first people you meet on a journey are omens, adumbrations, and no matter how you cut it, this is a bleak beginning that augurs ill for an adventure of my own devising, the walking of Broad Street, all thirteen miles of who-knows-what. It is something I never wanted to do when I lived here, but now, after residing in New York for a quarter century, it seems to be an essential exercise. I suppose I am searching for something. I don't know what. Or when. The past brings sorrow and the future anxiety, warn the Buddhists, so one concentrates on the moment. Can I keep my history cordoned off from the now, and hold the future at bay? These sofa salesmen, these sullen gray gents sipping on fumes and apprehension, are unable to come to grips with the impermanence of all things, most notably themselves. They are selling furniture to a world not very interested in furniture. I am wondering if this trek is the worst idea I ever concocted, if I am selling Philadelphia (or me) to a world (or me) not very interested in Philadelphia (or me). Aren't there important things for people to read about?

Maybe I just want to prove I can walk thirteen miles. I feel trim and frisky as I near sixty. Now that so many relatives have passed away and my visits to Philly are infrequent, maybe I need a reason to return to the old hometown to get reacquainted with some homeboys or rekindle my subterranean homesick blues. Hearing myself describe myself as "a kid from Philly" no longer surprises me, even though I haven't lived here for twenty-five years, since my twin boys were born, since we packed up and ran off to New York for fame and shelter from my mother, and now all I want to do is walk Broad Street, all of it, through the best and worst, through the blood and guts of North Philly, through the blight of Tioga, down the Avenue of the Arts, through Little Italy, past the stadia, and into the old Navy Yard, to see what's happened to it, to me, to us.

Those salesmen were me. Everyone I will encounter is me. Is that baby boomer perdition or Walt Whitman rapture?

I feel a funk coming on. It is not an unfamiliar sensation. I know what needs to be done: walk it off, exhaust the presentiment, unleash the endorphins, summon some distant knowledge that any trip, like any day, or any life, can begin inauspiciously and somehow end up swell. Or less than tragic.

The address of the northernmost house on Broad Street is 7206, which means City Hall is seventy-two blocks, approximately seven miles, due south, address of One, and then the numbers start to climb on the Southside. Philly is a city for idiots. Linear, rectangular, straight ahead. I love how they named all the nonnumbered streets in Center City after the trees they tore out to make room for the streets. Chestnut, Walnut, Cherry, Vine, Locust, Spruce. This row house at 7206 North Broad Street has been converted into a day care center called Leaps 'n' Bounds. Carolyn Pettigrew is looking after eight children between the ages of two and four. They are adorable tykes who need much looking after. You wish they were at home. Four, five, six hours is a long time for a toddler to be socializing away from home. Down the block, a larger, more colorful, more institutional day care center is under construction, Your Child's World. It is an offshoot of a facility that operates in another part of town. That one is open from 6 A.M. to 6 P.M. and some of the thirty kids spend ten hours a day at that place. Ten hours a day. You wish they were home and not there.

Know the child left behind.

That I will pass by another two dozen day care centers on Broad Street indicates that more and more mothers are working hard at jobs and more and more kids are working hard at being children without mothers.

Old men with no futures. Young kids with absentee mothers. This walk is off and limping. What could possibly come next? How about a funeral parlor? How about two?

Philadelphia Jews have an inexorable if clear-cut choice to make at the end of life and the beginning of Broad Street—Levine's Funeral Home or Goldstein Rosenberg Raphael-Sacks Inc. Of the fifteen funeral homes on Broad Street, the two for Jews are very close to each other geographically, financially, and spiritually. The veneer of secular harmony suddenly cracks in the face of the afterlife—for eternity, everyone wants to be with his own. Heaven must be segregated.

Goldstein Rosenberg Raphael-Sacks Inc. will be avoided today not because it sounds like a law firm or the result of a corporate merger, but because it was there where I last saw my mother. In her final repose. Five years ago. 'Round midnight. And it was a gargantuan error. Knowing she would not want to make such a long trip without photographs of her grandchildren, I went to Goldstein's to place a few snapshots in her plain spruce coffin ($550); she would have loved a pack of Pall Malls too, but I was hoping she was going to a no-smoking zone. She had smoked enough.

"This is not my mother," I said to no one in particular when I first saw her body in the wooden box. The two guards who had allowed me some private time pretended not to hear me from their safe distance in the hallway. "This is not my mother," I repeated, and took a few deep breaths, backed away, looked again, and then again, and was convinced that this corpse could not even pass for a Madame Tussaud version of my mother. They had made a grievous error. It happens. Hospitals dish out wrong babies to right parents, so why can't funeral homes dish out the wrong parent to the right son? Babies in cribs, old ladies in boxes. One group entering, one exiting. Near the end, almost all the old ladies, God knows, looked like my mother, matted white hair over hunched shoulders, timorous gaits behind metal walkers; how many times did I rush to help my mother cross a street even though she seldom ventured out of her apartment and I rarely came to Philadelphia? My mother's dotage and my guilt turned me into a Boy Scout. ("Rarely," by the way, was her word to describe my visitation frequency, which included every holiday, every birthday, every fall she took, every hip she cracked, every firing of a nurse, every new doctor, and every time she wound up in one of five local emergency rooms, which she considered a mini-chain of private clinics.)

I yelled for the guards. They pretended not to hear me. I went to the hallway to tell them about the mix-up face-to-face. They told me it was me who was mixed up. They showed me papers. Embarrassment rolled down my cheeks. A man ought to recognize his own mother, the woman who had given him life, had taught him the fundamentals of reading, writing, and Scotch-and-soda before sending him away to boarding school at the age of seven, and then invaded his psyche like an occupying army promising liberation and bringing chaos for decades.

Jews don't believe in viewings. They believe only God should see the dead. I stood there and shook and apologized through tears for not being a better son, more compassionate, more patient. I apologized for thwarting her suicide attempt. I apologized for everything I could think of that could be apologized for.

As I put the photographs into her casket, I wondered why the goyim put themselves through this kind of pain. Waiting for a resurrection? Making sure it's the right body being buried? Not a day goes by that I don't regret those moments, the last moments I ever saw my mother, lifeless, artificial, someone else.

By the time the guards came in to tell me it was time to go, I was smiling. I had remembered a joke. Not just any joke, but The Joke. I didn't want to, but I had no choice. The Joke was intended to be a commencement gift of sorts, as I was sixteen and had just graduated high school, the esteemed hellhole called Girard College, and my mother wanted me to know that she considered me a man. I had never heard The Joke before and have never heard it since, except in my own head. There are not many presents that stick with you for a half century, but this one had, and I replicate it now as accurately as possible, in spirit if not syllable:

Sarah and Nathan have been married fifty years. One day, they go for their annual checkups. The doctor has bad news. Sarah has an incurable disease, with only three months to live.

"What can I do for you, my precious Sarah?" asks Nathan when they arrive at home. "How can I make your last months more comfortable?"

"Well, Nathan, my sweet Nathan," says Sarah shyly, "just once before I die I would like to experience oral sex. Would you do that for me?"

"This is not my cup of tea," says Nathan, "but if this is your request, yes, of course."

A month later, Sarah and Nathan return to the doctor's office. After the examination, the doctor says to the couple, in a puzzled tone, "I don't know why, I don't know how, but Sarah has no signs of any disease whatsoever. She is one hundred percent healed."

At which point, Nathan slaps himself on the forehead and exclaims, "If only I had known this when my mother was sick!"

Yes, I will skip Goldstein Rosenberg Raphael-Sacks Inc. today and visit Levine's Funeral Home.

"How do people choose between these two funeral homes?" I ask.

"Based on their family history, their experience, their comfort level," says Joe Levine. "Everything else is very similar."

"Anything new in the business?"

"Graveside ceremonies and personalized eulogies are very popular," he says.

"Cremations?" I ask.

"You'll find more cremations in Denver and San Francisco than here," says Joe Levine. "We are a community of roots. Philadelphians live here and die here and have a need to be memorialized here so their families can visit. Jews get buried. We don't cremate."

There is no funeral today. Maybe no one died in a couple days. No Jews anyway. Joe Levine says more people die in the winter than in the summer, but he won't hazard a guess as to why. You have to think it's a combination of people missing their walks in the sun, and caretakers unable to get to work through snowdrifts, and cranky doctors who miss their golf games, and just old-fashioned poetic justice. Philadelphia winters are for dying.

"How long you been here at 7100 Broad Street?"

"We've been here at 7100 North Broad for a half century," says Joe Levine.

"And before that?"

"Fifteen twelve North Broad Street."

"You're very loyal to Broad Street."

"Like they say in real estate," says Joe Levine, "location, location, location. Broad Street gives us visibility and accessibility. Everybody knows where Broad Street is."

In a manner of speaking, funeral parlors are in the real estate game. Whenever a cemetery opens, funeral homes purchase any number of plots, so that, in the event someone hasn't planned well, a funeral director, like Joe Levine, can, on the spot, sell a place to spend eternity. Catholic funeral homes don't enjoy this side business: the churches own the cemeteries.

"A couple years ago," says Joe Levine, "a golden opportunity came our way, and we purchased the whole of Salomon Memorial Park in Frazer, Pennsylvania."

"You know who Haym Salomon is?" I ask.

"Excuse me," says Joe Levine, and takes a phone call.

Haym Salomon was an immigrant businessman who spoke eight languages and became known as the Financier of the Revolution. Many experts think he wrote the first draft of the U.S. Constitution. Some think he designed the Great Seal of the United States, explaining the thirteen colonies arranged in a Star of David above the eagle's head. Salomon died penniless and was buried without a marker in any language in a Jewish cemetery in Center City Philadelphia.

"According to state law," says Joe Levine, "anyone can be a plot purveyor and buy twenty or fifty or a hundred cemetery plots and then resell them." The reason is for family togetherness; maybe you want a big family picnic in perpetuity, maybe you've had it with noisy neighbors. And then maybe someone in your family changes their mind or gets a divorce and decides to sell the plots. You can. At a profit. One at a time or in bulk.

"Sounds like an interesting business venture, Joe," I say.

"I'm not worried," says Joe Levine. "Only funeral homes have the opportunity to resell the plots."

"Ever hear of eBay, Joe?"

I call my brother on the cell phone as I continue to walk.

"Wanna corner the market on cemetery plots?" I ask.

"Are you sick?" he asks.

"You don't like the idea?" I ask.

"I'm still asleep," he says.

"Then you might like the idea when you wake up?"

"Buying and selling cemetery plots?" he asks.

"Yes."

"No. It's too creepy," he says.

"Very little competition," I say.

"Because it's too creepy," he repeats.

"You'll be the only one on craigslist or eBay."

"Because it's too damn creepy."

"All the aging baby boomers guarantee a spike in sales in the near future."

"Can I have some coffee before we talk about dying baby boomers?"

It is very early in Santa Monica, California, and my brother has not had his Peet's yet. I call him nowadays with business ideas even though I have no intention of ever following through, and doubt he will either, but I hang on to the remote chance that one notion will grab his fancy and he'll follow through and find his true calling and make a killing and live the good life and thank me. My baby brother, fifty-six, has owned a mail order business, a video business, and a publishing business; he can sell anything he sets his mind to selling: books on the Internet, antique French posters, blue-green algae, or movies directed by Robert Downey Sr. He is a charming Sagittarian who often gets offered overpriced drinks in moodily lit bars when he's mistaken for Richard Gere; he cannot cash in on his doppelgänger-ness, since he is in his twelfth year of sobriety. He graduated Betty Ford with honors. He is an undergraduate at Antioch and a full-time drug counselor; big headaches, small wages.

"Where are you?" asks my brother.

"City of Brotherly Love, brother."

"Why?"

"I'm walking Broad Street, from one end to the other."

"You're what?" he asks.

"Walking Broad Street. From Cheltenham Avenue to the Delaware River."

"You lose a bet?"

"No. I volunteered."

"Why?" he wants to know.

"I don't know. Maybe I missed something when we lived here."

"I know what you'll miss soon enough," he says.

"What's that?"

"The three Cs."

"Three Cs?" I repeat.

"Cops, cabs, and Caucasians."

"You think it's dangerous?" I ask.

"Dangerous?" he repeats. "Let me tell you how dangerous. I'm willing to sell you a cemetery plot half price, right now."

"You really think it's dangerous?"

"Call me when you get to Girard Avenue. If you're still alive."

"You're very reassuring," I say.

"I gotta get some coffee," he says.

He has reason to worry. More people were murdered in 2005 in Philadelphia than in Cleveland, Pittsburgh, San Jose, and San Diego combined. Philadelphia ranked number one in the nation in murders per capita. Still, on average, only one person a day gets killed in Philly, and that person is usually young, usually black, usually involved in some crazy drama involving girlfriends or gangs or vague disrespect. I don't like the numbers, but I like my odds. I'd like some coffee too.

The white letters atop the Oak Lane Diner's roof are seven feet high and virtually belt, Ethel Merman–style, "Welcome to Phila-del-phia!" It is a classic diner, all shiny chrome and stainless steel and black and white tiles and clean countertops and booths and sassy waitresses who serve homemade pies baked on the premises daily, which does not make them better or worse than other pies, just part of the institution that has been here at Broad and 66th Avenue for sixty-six years.

You would know the city by the breakfast side dishes: only $2.35 for bacon, sausage, ham, or scrapple. Scrapple. Unlike cheesesteaks and hoagies and oversized soft pretzels, scrapple is one of Philadelphia's culinary delights that has not caught on nationally. Ingredients, not taste, are at the root of the circumscribed distribution: hog skin, hog heart, hog liver, hog tongue, hog brains, any old offal or entrails, hog lips, hog testes, hog neck bones, hog ears, and meat scraped from hog heads. The frugal Pennsylvania Dutch used every inch of the pig except the squeal; they couldn't bear to discard any leftovers from the butchering, so they held all the umbles together in a loaf with cornmeal, flour, water, thyme, sage, and strong black pepper. If you cut a slice, flour it properly, and fry it up just right, it rivals any breakfast meat on earth. To hell with haggis.

With ketchup dappled on my sunny-side-up eggs, my home fries, and my scrapple, North Broad tastes like heaven, or a shortcut to it.

Sipping coffee in a Philly diner without a *Daily News* is a misfeasance. Today's tabloid features items about union unrest, John Street, Larry Bowa, Bruce Springsteen, DA Lynne Abraham, restaurateur Neil Stein, Eagle madness, Governor Ed Rendell, DJ Jerry Blavat, Dick Vermeil, Senator Arlen Specter, and the dismissal of the Cardinal Dougherty High School athletic director for using racist epithets. He used the N-word twice while addressing his young football team. Twenty-five years and nothing has changed. Same people, same plights, same biases, same newspaper. Arlen Specter was a DA running for the Senate when I left. Lynne Abraham was a hanging judge who wanted to be DA. Larry Bowa was on the Phillies. Mayor John Street was just elected to the City Council, after working his way through Temple Law School by selling hot dogs on the street. These same names are still news. Is this the Twilight Zone edition of the *Daily News*? No, it's just Philadelphia. Nothing and nobody changes.

It's comforting; it's disconcerting. It's why you left twenty-five years ago; it's why you are back today.

Philly is a small town hiding in a big city.

Philly is a big town masquerading as a small city.

Philly is Baltimore on steroids.

Philly is a bathroom break between NYC and DC.

Philly is an archipelago whose islands are surrounded by concrete.

In a nation of Toll Brothers' computer-generated neighborhoods, of million-dollar LEGO mansions in gated communities, Philadelphia is authentic—a hardcore city with genuine neighborhoods, and those hoods are as distinct, as idiosyncratic, and as competitive as the equestrian clubs that race the Palio in Siena. It is not a farrago of faux streets and ersatz manses designed to sell fast, it's a real place with real people, mean streets and mean streaks, and music that no one else in the world cares about pours from row houses and hospital waiting rooms. "Open My Eyes" by the Nazz or "The 81" by Candy and the Kisses. It's home. No one pretends Philadelphia is a land of milk and honey—more like Yuengling and Tastykakes—but its provenance cannot be denied, with its own cuisine and parlance, its own quirks and quarks and tastes, and Bill Conlin too, a crotchety history buff of a sports columnist whose two cents are worth four bits any day.

After breezing through the *Daily News,* you pick up the *Philadelphia Inquirer,* once a great paper, now suffering financial and editorial convulsions, searching for a new reason to be, and the means to be it. Here's a column by Tom Ferrick Jr. He was my editor when I wrote for the *Temple News* sometime in the last century. Damned if he isn't writing about walking Broad Street to work every day. He has a wry wit, a mature voice. Ferrick was always mature. Too mature for me. We weren't the best of friends, but I should stop by and see ol' Tom when I get downtown, talk about the passage of time and walking B. Street. That'll be nice. That he hasn't traveled very far since college is no surprise; that's the Philadelphia dance of life—a straight path that somehow leads back to where it started. Like a line dance on *Ameri-*

can Bandstand, or at a Jerry Blavat hop. You grow up in a neighbor-hood, attend Temple or Penn or La Salle or Villanova or Drexel or St. Joe's, move to Center City or the hippest hood of the moment, get a career going, drink at Dirty Frank's, play the field until you find a suitable mate, and then move to the burbs or back to the hood, or the burbs nearest the hood, or the hood nearest the burbs.

Tom Ferrick Jr. was born in Philly, went to Temple University (on Broad Street), and has worked at the *Inquirer* (on Broad Street) ever since. He will tell you that Philadelphians are the least likely folks in America to move away from their hometown, and not because they have been dropped into Valhalla, not by a long shot; in fact, Philadel-phians are perpetually mildly depressed and almost happy to be so. Lex loci. Even Tom Ferrick Jr., hometown hero, had to confess in one column:

"I was born in Philadelphia in 1949, and, shortly thereafter, the city began a half century of decline. I swear, it wasn't my fault. . . . Even if you were born with the sunniest of dispositions (and my mother swears I was) . . . pessimism seeps into your psyche.

"Combine this pessimism with the city's centuries-old inferiority complex, add a cup and a half of cynicism, and you have the Philadel-phia state of mind. It's a belief system that states that the only reason these aren't the worst of times is because the future is going to be even more terrible."

And Ferrick is the brightest, bounciest columnist in town!

Home again, home again, dancing the jig!

(Note to fact checker: that business about Philadelphians being the least likely folks to move away—don't bother trying to verify that fact, for no such records are kept by the census or anyone with any senses. I have wasted many hours in that fruitless pursuit. It's just an article of faith around here and no one wants to be disabused of that unprovable proposition. Home again, home again, jiggety jog. Who knows why we're so high on the hog? Cherry water ice? The boat-houses near the Museum of Art bathed in crepuscular light? The

Phillies? Yo, staying home ain't always an indication of contentment.)

I have an old friend who went to an All-Star fantasy camp to play hardball with some childhood memories. What he took away from that camp was neither pitching in the big game nor receiving personalized hitting instructions from Gary Matthews Sr., but the bizarre behavior of fellow campers. His hackles went up when he first heard someone yell, "Nice pitch!" or "Way to go!" He thought they were being sarcastic. Which is only natural in Philadelphia. Then he heard these "taunts" again and again—"Good effort!" "Bad luck!" "We'll get 'em next time!" It took him all week to realize these digs were unambiguously sincere, were paroxysms of support, something heretofore foreign to him. No spitters, no scroogies, just people being nice. Pathologically nice! He concluded that people from places other than Philadelphia were a different breed. And they gave him the willies. You meet anyone from the Philadelphia diaspora anywhere in the world and there is an instant bond, a sense of belonging to a very tight if unharmonious tribe. Santa Monicans don't have that. Syracusians don't either. Philadelphians do.

Outside the Oaklane Diner, a black and tan squirrel is schlepping a drumstick across the parking lot. I follow him (or her). Squirrels like nuts, and seeds and fungi and buds and leaves and stuff like that. They are known to be vegetarians. Sure, urban squirrels settle for stale pizza in a pinch, but they pass on the pepperoni. Squirrels have to watch their salt intake, or their heart rate and blood pressure go crazy and shorten their already short little lives. Tough gig, finding unsalted scraps in a diner's garbage. So I follow this flexitarian squirrel, and watch him (or her) climb a fence in the parking lot, find a comfortable spot, and munch serenely on the drumstick. Not just the breading either, but the meat. Maybe she's pregnant. If I had forty-four days, I could wait and see. Maybe I will. I just stand and watch. I can feel her (his) heart racing. I can feel mine racing in sympathy. No kidding. I have atrial fibrillation. I half expected to see myself reflected in the eyes and lives of strangers, of morticians, sofa salesmen, teachers, waitresses, tailors, vagabonds, sure, but not squirrels. My pulse is elevating and I hurriedly check my shoulder bag for the medication. I find pens, pads, a stopwatch, a brochure from Gordon's Furniture, Vioxx, Tylenol, Valium, Mineral, Ice, Vaseline, Lanoxin, Lomotrin, Pepto-Bismol, and a one-gulp airplane bottle of Wild Turkey. Who knows what thirteen miles of bad road may bring? The Vioxx is a souvenir. I stopped taking it when news reports said it caused strokes and heart attacks. The day the drug was withdrawn from the market, Merck's stock dropped 25 percent in a single day, causing, possibly, as many strokes and embolisms as the drug itself. A deluge of lawsuits ensued. One has to wonder how many witnesses in how many courtrooms will testify for or against Vioxx without the benefit of some other Merck pharmaceutical coursing through their systems.

The squirrel has finished her drumstick. If she had a little napkin, she would dab the corners of her mouth. She enjoyed her drumstick. She just sits on the fence, next to a familiar unnerving green sign:

LEW BLUM TOWING
1130 N 40th St.
222-5628 $150/15 a day storage
CASH ONLY

In a recent straw poll, Philadelphians voted for the most notorious Philadelphians of all time. The top five were: Ira Einhorn (the hippie whose shiksa girlfriend was found in a trunk in his apartment before he went on the lam for twenty years); Gary Heidnik (who murdered two women and then raped and tortured three more before chaining them to his basement wall and forcing them to eat the first two women); Frank Rizzo (the brutal police chief of the 1960s who volunteered his police department to invade Cuba before he became the brutal mayor of the 1970s); Mumia Abu-Jamal (a writer and political activist convicted of the murder of a police officer in 1981 who has since become a cause célèbre for both opponents and supporters of the death penalty); and Lew Blum.

(Bob Saget got a few votes just for being Bob Saget. Bill Cosby, as much an embarrassment as an icon nowadays, earned some votes not only for lashing out against ebonics and the hip-hop nation, but for claims of sexual improprieties on his part, involving roofies, followed by the fondling of unconscious women.)

I call Lew Blum. They will get him for me, no questions asked. Philadelphians may not be polite, but they are not ashamed of themselves.

"Lew Blum," says Lew Blum.

"How many cars do you tow every day?" I ask.

"I can't tell you that," he says.

"Why not?"

"That's my whole business, right there. What else?"

"How many signs do you have around the city?" I ask.

"I can't tell you that, then my competitors will know. What else?"

"How many competitors do you have?" I ask.

"Too many. I'm third-generation towing and trust me, this used to be much easier. My grandfather was Lew Smith, my uncle was George Smith, my mother's married name is Blum. You know who tows the most vehicles? The Philadelphia Parking Authority. A hundred cars a day, easy. And you know why? They don't play fair. They put up signs about six inches by ten inches, and you can't even see them. The private tow guys, we have to put up signs three feet by three feet. Hey, let me have teeny-weeny signs and I'll tow a hundred cars a day too. People should complain about the Parking Authority, not me."

"How big are their signs really?" I ask.

"Okay, maybe ten by twelve, but I'm being generous."

"How many vehicles do you tow a day?"

"You already asked me that. You think I forgot already?"

"How many employees do you have?" I ask.

"I have enough to get the job done. Just enough drivers, towers, and salespeople."

"Salespeople?"

"Salespeople. How do you think I get business? I go to a Rite Aid and say, 'Let me put up a sign and I'll take care of your parking lot, keep it clean, keep it legit, get rid of the riffraff.' I have salespeople doing that. And then we patrol. Just yesterday, a woman parks at KFC and goes in and eats her chicken and then decides to go shopping down the street. No good, lady. We tow her. She says she was in the KFC. Sure, lady. We have patrols who count the parking lot cars and then go in and count the customers. We go to the manager. If there are ten cars and only seven customers, we tow three. Oh, you were in the bathroom, lady? Bullshit! We sent a woman into the ladies' room and you weren't there. We sent a man into the men's room and you weren't there either. Try another story, lady."

"How many cars do you tow a day?"

"Again with that question? Let's say I tow eight to ten cars a day. That sounds good. We patrol Rite Aid and 7-Eleven and driveways and empty lots and we don't get paid by the establishment, only by the cars we tow. People should understand that."

"How many signs do you have around town?" I ask.

"Again? Let's say five thousand to seven thousand signs in Philadelphia. That sounds good. If you don't have an authorized vehicle, we'll get you. And that includes cars with handicap stickers too. Those people want it both ways. First, they cry that they want to be equal, equal this and equal that, and then you tow their cars and suddenly they are privileged characters. Well, I don't play that game. If you are unauthorized, you get towed. Things don't always work out the way you planned."

"Thank you," I say.

"For what?" asks Lew Blum.

"For answering my questions," I say.

"You think I answered your questions?" asks Lew Blum.

The squirrel is gone. She must have climbed down the fence and scurried off to her dray whilst I was taking notes. She must have run across the graffito that says: "It's Lew Blum's world and we just park in it."

Across the street from the diner is the Halal Bilal Steak-and-Take Drive-Thru, a clean well-lighted fast food joint for Muslims. In Arabic, "halal" means lawful or permitted, which the following foods and beverages are not: alcohol and intoxicants, blood, blood by-products, swine, carnivorous animals, animals dead before slaughtering, birds of prey, and land animals without external ears, such as snakes and other descendants of dinosaurs. Scrapple will not be on the menu.

But you can watch the female cooks in full chadors prepare a Muslim Hoagie with five kinds of turkey instead of salami and cappicola, and Lamb Cheesesteak with the works, fried onions, peppers, and mushrooms. Yams and collard greens are sides. The Italian water ices are Mali Mango, Congo Cherry, Libya Lemon, Rasta Raspberry, Watusi Pineapple Coconut, and Guinea Grape. You could not get away with Guinea Grape in South Philly.

Hassan Stevens, a big dude who should probably cut down on the intake of his own product, owns and operates the Halal Bilal Steak-and-Take Drive-Thru. His family owns three others, with more on the way because there are 200,000 Muslims in Philly, with more on the way. Through conversion and immigration, best estimates stand at three to four million Muslims across the country. "At current rates of increase," according to the American Society of Muslims, "there will be more Muslims than Presbyterians within the decade. Early in this century their numbers may well grow past six million, at which point there will be more American Muslims than Jews."

Six million is a touchy number for Jews.

"I go to a farm in Virginia every week," says Hassan exuberantly.

"When I find the animals I want, I have to pacify them, rub their heads, get friendly with them before they get slaughtered or they'd be tough meat. If they get tense, if I have to chase them around, I just let them go. Cows, lamb, no difference. Let 'em go."

"And when they are calm?" I ask.

"When the animal is calm, I say a prayer in Arabic—in the name of Allah—and slit the animal's throat, and then I have fifteen seconds to get the animal into the slaughterhouse before he wakes up and causes all kinds of trouble. A cow can be very strong, as strong as a . . . a . . ."

"A bull?" I say.

"Yes. A bull! The slit just knocks them out for a little bit. The slaughterhouse does the rest and I bring them back to Broad Street and break them down and we have the freshest, cleanest meat you can find anywhere. All according to halal laws."

Bilal was the constant companion of Prophet Muhammad. He remained faithful to his teacher while going through unspeakable crimes at the hands of infidels. Bilal always had a special place in the Muslim heart, but especially during these crusader days, these dark days of invaders and renditions and prisoners at Gitmo Bay, Cuba. *Cuanto mas cambia, mas es la misma cosa.*

Hassan Stevens's family is Sunni, the minority sect in Iraq and the majority in Islam. They attend a large mosque that considers itself moderate. Muslims, like Christians, evangelize the world over and look forward to converting the human race to their faith since they have the ear of the Lord and the sole pipeline to Heaven—that place of magnificence that comes after a lifetime of poverty. Stevens's father was a Black Muslim before the fragmentation of the Nation of Islam, before Louis Farrakhan broke with Elijah Muhammad's son, Imam W. Dean Mohammed, aka Honorable Wallace D. Mohammed, aka Warith D. Mohammed, aka W. D. Mohammed.

You want to understand what's going on in the Muslim community, so you buy a copy of the *Final Call*, Louis Farrakhan's newspaper, which sits on the Halal Bilal countertop. In forty pages, you will find thirty-one photographs of Minister Louis Farrakhan, twenty-seven mentions of his name, plus schedules for his radio shows, television appearances, and live speeches, as well as adverts for CDs, DVDs, and tapes, including your choice of Minister Louis Farrakhan performing violin concertos of Beethoven (CD only) or Felix Mendelssohn (VHS only).

Louis Farrakhan is the winner of the award for most self-aggrandizing publisher in history, barely beating out Oprah Winfrey. Oprah, who in her youth must have thought being on a cover was a cruel pipe dream, has been on all seventy-five covers of *O* magazine since its launch in 2000. Oprah will remain *O*'s exclusive cover girl for the foreseeable and distant future. Come the month when Oprah is not on the cover of *O*, she will magically turn that into a publicity event, an act of magnanimity.

O, Allah, what will satisfy these good folks? When will enough be enough? Ben Franklin may have quoted himself a lot and made a lot of money from his pamphlet, but he had the modesty or devilry or business moxie to write under pseudonyms and call his publication *Poor Richard's Almanack*. It ran for twenty-five years. That he was postmaster general didn't hurt. Guess whose pamphlets and newspapers always were delivered first.

"What's your biggest seller?" I ask Hassan.

"We go through 7,500 pounds of whiting every week."

"Do you kill the fish a special way?"

"Sunnis consider all fish halal, if you don't find them dead."

"And business goes well?" I ask.

"Muslims have a duty to eat here," says Hassan.

"How come?"

"Muslims are not supposed to walk by a halal restaurant. It may cost a little more, but they understand our steak sandwiches are clean, all beef, and our fish is fresh."

I look around the Steak-and-Take. "How come business doesn't look so hot, Hassan?"

"It's Ramadan," says Hassan.

"Oy, vey," I say. "Salaam aleichem."

Block after block, there are large houses with tasteful front yards and a car parked right in front of each home. No pedestrians are found on this uncluttered, leafy part of Broad Street. I guess everyone is at work. I try to convince myself that I too am at work. Writers are always trying to convince themselves that whatever they are doing is work, that they are not really a self-involved, self-deluded, self-isolating, self-serving, self-abnegating, self-reverential, self-redundant bunch who, barely moving from a keyboard, transform a paucity of other talents into a passion for something they swear destiny had in store for them all along. Maybe that's why I am walking. I suddenly remember I don't like walking. Never did like it and never do it except when the dog demands it and then I love watching her walk, or run circles around me, then hippety-hop after rabbits, disappear and reappear from the flora in her golden saunter, chase rodents and squirrels up and down holes and trees. So free to follow her instincts, yet so steadfast, the way writers try to be. I think of sentences while she walks, and remember pledges I have broken. The daily hour in the park with the dog makes me more human, less self-absorbed.

Tacked on trees and telephone poles around Chelten Avenue are tacky 8½ x 11 inch sheets of paper that read: "888-821-1958 . . . work from home . . . earn serious money." A prerecorded voice tells me to leave my name and number and the best time to call back if I want to earn more than $1,000 per month for only ten hours a week of work from my home. I leave my name and number and best times to reach me. Anytime. Night or day. I am home a lot. I wish I were there now. I feel unqualified for the unspecified job on the telephone pole even before I speak to the unknown employer.

Now a FOR SALE sign on a front lawn grabs your attention. It too displays a telephone number. You call. Why not? Without identifying the real estate company, the voice asks you to press number 5 if you are interested in "this elegant stone single home with five bedrooms, three and a half bathrooms, hardwood floors throughout, a renovated kitchen, finished basement, new boiler, a detached garage, a terrace on a quarter acre of land, for only $329,900. If you are prequalified for a mortgage, leave your name and number. If not, we have a deal for you . . . for your dream home . . . no complicated forms, no banks . . . call now."

I already called. I look at the cell phone. You'd think financing for an elegant $330,000 dream home would require some complicated forms and bank involvement, particularly if you are not prequalified. I am not prequalified. I don't think. I don't know what that means. I know the median value of a dwelling in Philly is $60,700 and the median income for a household is about half that, or $31,000. Almost a quarter of the population of Philadelphia is below the poverty line, even if that poverty line is a jagged, vacillating, fault-filled, and relativistic thing. Poverty is usually defined as households that earn less than 25 percent of the median income of a particular community. In this case, the poverty line is $7,750.

Almost a quarter of the population of Philadelphia is making less than a quarter of the median income. Five'll getcha ten that that spells misery for a great number of folks.

NO CHILD LEFT

Stenton Avenue to Champlost Street

A T the four corners of Broad and Stenton are three gas stations and a U.S. Post Office. As a student at Temple University, I worked the night shift at the main post office, loading and unloading trucks with sixty-pound mailbags. One night, a substitute supervisor was taking roll when he stopped at my name and asked if I knew a Moe Buschel. I did not. He told me he once worked with a big guy named Moe, thought he might be a relative. Sorry.

A couple hours into my graveyard shift, the supervisor came over to ask again. He described the man as tall, mustachioed, a really kind man when he wasn't arm wrestling everyone into submission.

"He died young," said the supervisor. "On his way home one night after work."

"Was his real name Morris?" I asked.

"Yes," he said. "That's him. Morris. We called him Moe."

"Oh. I never knew he had a nickname."

"So, you knew him?"

"He was my father."

• • •

Always challenged by word puzzles, I study the brainteaser that is on the large sign at the Exxon station across the street:

> to ch free   ar wa h
> $1 of wit   gas pur
> loter   moord
> $4   ater $5 water & w x 6 under

Following serious contemplation, I approach the man in the Exxon office.

"Hello," I say.

"Do you want gasoline?" he asks in a Hindi accent.

"No thank you. What does your sign say?"

"You don't want gasoline?" he asks again.

"I don't have a car," I say. "What does your sign say?"

"Can you not read?" he asks.

"Yes, I can read," I say.

"Then go and read the sign and leave me alone."

"But I can't read your sign," I say.

"Then just go," he says and waves his hand as if throwing an invisible Frisbee.

His disposition is familiarly phlegmatic, but the accent may not in fact be Hindi. It could be Urdu or Bengali or Farsi or Pashto or any number of languages from any number of nations. He could be Indian or Far Eastern or Filipino or Malaysian or any combination of those and more. I am too ignorant to know and too embarrassed to inquire. He could have arrived here last week or last generation. Small matter. He is a Philadelphian now. As far from sanguine as it gets.

High blood pressure and an aggressively defensive posture are required now, looking for an ace up every sleeve, a scam down every pant leg, and then secretly feeling guilty for such hypervigilance, yet more than willing to mete out maledictions to cover any miscalculations. Cracking wise is a green card, fulmination a passport.

Philadelphians are not polite people. Candid, perhaps, brusque, you bet, but polite? It's just not a high priority, cuz. Honesty trumps niceness. Brevity bests bullshit. Philadelphians would rather be smart or dismissive or wiseass or informative. Harrisburgers and New Hopers are on their toes when they come to the big city. Philadelphians are fast talkers and fast thinkers (think Chris Matthews and Jim Cramer) and no one has time for chitchat or palaver, unless it's time designated for chitchat or palaver. Everyone is busy doing something even if you can't tell what it is they are busy doing.

If the person selling you a cup of coffee in the morning throws in a "Have a nice day," that person is from elsewhere, from Allentown or Arizona. Philadelphians don't appreciate nice days forced down their throats; it stimulates their gag reflex. Philadelphians are more philosophical, not to say miasmic, about good days. Some are good, most ain't, what can you do? There are no polemics attached to this outlook, just a dogged acceptance akin to Muscovites welcoming winter by hunkering down with Stolichnaya and Solzhenitsyn instead of bitching and moaning and watching the Weather Channel compulsively, and then ordering Micro Twill Gore-Tex poly Patagonia underwear online.

Don't get me wrong: Philadelphians are not curmudgeons. They are capable of kind acts and charitable deeds. Take Zell Kravinsky. After the real estate maven discovered that giving away $35 million did not satisfy his altruistic urge, and even though his wife, a psychiatrist, thought him crazy and threatened to divorce him on those very grounds, one morning, predawn, he snuck past his sleeping wife and four sleeping kids and checked into Einstein Medical Center to have his right kidney removed and placed into a stranger in the adjacent room.

Not even Zell Kravinsky—humanitarian, philanthropist, socialist—puts much stock in politesse. Nice is not a goal.

Authenticity, not superiority, is what Philadelphians take pride in. No razzle-dazzle for the tourists or the neighbors. It's a throwback city, like a primo Mitchell & Ness jersey; something nostalgic, something uplifting, something from a better time, when everything had meaning, when loyalty was extant, when the bottom line didn't always include a dollar sign. The Mummers Parade—the annual New Year's Day celebration where 15,000 locals strut north on South Broad—remains the largest and weirdest unsponsored event in America. One hundred years plus. No corporations invited. No logos allowed. It ain't for the bucks, bub, it's for the tradition, and to honor all the tough guys who dress up like women, the guys who strum banjos and bang glockenspiels, who strut their stuff through the freezing winds, tacking their feathery headdresses and shouldering elaborately sequined costumes, transforming day laborers into cakewalking double-decker ice cream cones with neon sprinkles. At its best, a club presents an entire Broadway musical in five mobile minutes, from *The King and I* to *The Lion King*. Up to 100,000 people brave the weather for the thrill of tradition, the watering of the roots (with beer), the intoxication of belonging somewhere real. It's Mardi Gras without the tits.

Broad and Champlost must be the result of clever planning or dark humor. The 35th Police Precinct, North Detective District, is directly across the street from Dunkin' Donuts, saving time and shoe-leather for the cops, two of whom are presently hanging out in front of the station, catching a smoke. I ought to talk to the cops, just for the heck of it, see what's up. As I approach them, I feel awash in guilt, of something, of anything. I check my pockets for pot. I check my soul for misdemeanors. I think I see one of them whisper into a walkie-talkie: "The perp is a middle-aged male Caucasian, medium height, medium build, white mustache, blue jeans, dark baseball cap, black Mephisto boots, 4E width, a secondhand black French work jacket from I. Goldberg, pockets filled with barely legible annotations, cheap Bic pens lifted from different hotels, and a full slate of regrets. Roger that."

Philly cops give me the willies. I can't help it. Frank Rizzo's Reign of Terror still nips at my soul. He was larger than life as police chief, then as mayor, later as legend. He ran the city with an iron billy club. Every time you lit a joint or marched in a protest, you looked over your shoulder for Frank Rizzo—not an apparition or representative of Frank Rizzo, but the man himself. His outsized charisma delighted the angry white row-home owners and turned the words "law and order" into a code for all things demagogue. Frank Rizzo was Philly personified: a tough-talking, grammatically challenged paisano who came from the streets and preferred the gutters. He was Rocky with a badge. He made you root for the criminals.

Truth is, he formed a secret police force to investigate political opponents during the 1971 mayoral campaign. He was our Nixon, minus Watergate, and like Nixon, the courts later confirmed most of the citizenry's worst suspicions and fears. In 1979, the U.S. District Court charged that Rizzo and eighteen high-ranking city and police officials either committed or condoned "widespread and severe" acts of police brutality, tolerating beatings and shootings of suspects.

Atrocious favoritism and racism by both the police and fire departments—brother Joe Rizzo was fire commissioner—instigated federal lawsuits that led to affirmative action in civil service hirings and promotions.

But Frank Rizzo liked being emperor. When he tried to rewrite the city charter in order to run for a third term as mayor, he stood naked. Even his admirers saw his ambitious dingle dangling. The citizenry dressed him down. He was gone.

Today, his son, Frank Jr., who easily won councilman at large elections in 1999 and 2003, is preparing to run for mayor in 2007. It will have a gruesomely familiar ring, Mayor Rizzo. It's why you left; it's why you are back. The more Philly changes, the more it stays the same.

Più il Philly cambia, il più che rimane lo stesso.

On the third corner of Broad and Champlost is a Wendy's. A Wendy's Baked Potato with Chili and Cheese has more calories and more fat than a McDonald's Quarter Pounder with Cheese. But a Wendy's Cheeseburger has less fat and fewer calories than a Burger

King Tender Crisp Garden Salad with Garden Ranch Dressing. You
have to get up early in the morning to get more unhealthy than the
McDonald's Deluxe Breakfast—at 1,220 calories, 61 grams of fat, 17
grams of saturated fat, and 480 milligrams of cholesterol, it serves up
more damage than anything you have eaten since that foie gras and
scrapple sandwich served with a side of schmaltz.

Speaking of schmaltz, on the fourth corner of Broad and Champlost is a Blockbuster Video. It smells like all Blockbusters smell after
a recent carpet cleaning: minty/lemony/aerosolly/toxic. The counterfeit gangsta behind the register is eyeballing me.

"Can I ask you a question?" I ask.

"Whachew wan', man?" he asks.

"What movie rents the most at this store?" I ask.

"Fuck if I know," says the kid.

"What movie sells the most at this store?" I ask.

"Whachew wan' here, man?" he snarls.

This is what I want: I want to see a real gangster movie in a real
movie theater, not a gangsta saleskid at some smelly Blockbuster. Fact
is, I want all Blockbusters to vanish, to go the way of Betamax, poof,
gone, history, just like all the movie theaters on Broad Street. Thirteen
miles of prime commercial real estate, and not a single movie house
left standing, zero, and I'm holding you personally responsible, kid,
and don't tell me it ain't fair 'cause life ain't fair and genuine gangstas
know that. Now you make all my dreams come true or I'll blow your
fucking head off.

Then he would say, in my filmic fantasy, Wait a minute, mister, I
didn't mean no harm. I'm just trying to make some money and help
out my poor mama. And then we'd sit down and I'd tell him stories
about growing up around here with three movie theaters on three
consecutive blocks, all with balconies and double features, and how I
used to walk from my home to Broad Street to see *The Dirty Dozen* or
A Thousand Clowns or Gina Lollobrigida's two buoyant breasts float-

ing on the bubbles of her bathwater, submerged just enough to hide her dark Roman nipples. The Lane was the art house on Broad Street where I saw black and white French films and angry English dramas about depraved soccer players and horny long-distance runners and doomed interracial couples, dark grainy movies that illuminated the tragedies of our irretrievably human condition. That's what I want, kid, and pronto. You down wit dat?

"I got a history of violence," the kid says.

"I'm not surprised," I say.

"The movie, man, the movie."

"Oh."

"All 'bout Phillufya. Y'ever see it?"

Indeed. *A History of Violence* is about members of the Philly mob hunting down Super Viggo Mortensen so they can kill him. Fat chance. Director David Cronenberg has said, "In the graphic novel, it's the New York mob, but Josh Olson [the screenwriter] is from Philly, so he changed it to his hometown. I liked that because I wanted them all to be second-rate mobsters, not the top guys."

Right, top guys like Scorsese's doomed psychos or the Sopranos who couldn't shoot straight. What does that Canadian know about the Philly mob anyway? I call Josh Olson. He says he moved the characters to Philly because knowing the streets and the vernacular meant less research, and he could visit his old stompin' grounds. Writers are lazy, he says, and directors are full of shit.

"Brian De Palma is from Philly, and *Blow Out* drove me nuts. Such lies. He had Travolta driving through City Hall, when you can't do that, and then he runs out of the 30th Street Station and he's on 15th Street! Drove me nuts.

"M. Night Shyamalan shoots in Philly, he uses the locations beautifully, but his films are not about Philadelphia. Not in the way Barry Levinson's are about Baltimore. I guess you could say Baltimore is to Philly what Philly is to New York.

"The only really smart thing I ever did concerning Philadelphia was leave. People never leave. My friends are doing very well, but they either never left or they left for a while and returned. Something about that place you can't shake. I'm from Powelton Village and my best friend is still there. I remember when the police had a machine gun trained on him from a rooftop during the MOVE siege. You don't forget stuff like that, when the police burn down your neighborhood. My mother still lives in Philly. You know, if you misquote me . . . or make me look bad . . . I'll hunt you down . . . and kill you."

Beat-2-3. Whoa. Is he kidding? Is this a Hollywood negotiation tactic? All I really know is that the man who wrote *A History of Violence* is threatening to hunt me down and kill me. I saw the movie. Twice. He must be kidding, right? Philadelphians have a sick sense of humor, and you never know when one is joshin', even if he lives in Hollywood and that's his name. I tell him I have another call coming in.

If you don't know about the MOVE siege, here is a quick history of violence, essential for the understanding of Philadelphia. Back in the 1980s, there was a revolutionary group called MOVE, mostly African-American back-to-nature buffs who were anti-technology, anti-authority, and antisocial. They wore dreadlocks and bathed infrequently. Sometimes, they preached through bullhorns for hours and upset their neighbors. They lived communally in a large house in the middle of a middle-class street in a middle-class neighborhood. They were not pacifists. A decade before, during a confrontation with the police, a cop was killed and MOVE members were convicted.

In 1985, one summer day, the police reported a shootout with MOVE, claiming the group was firing automatic weapons. No one was hurt, but that evening, a state police helicopter dropped a C4 bomb, packed in a satchel resembling a child's bookbag, on the roof of the MOVE house, and Philly police shot ten thousand rounds of ammunition into the residence. Eleven MOVE members were murdered. Sixty houses were burned to the ground. The police chief said it was his idea to drop the bomb. The mayor said he okayed the bomb. The fire chief said it was his idea to let the fire burn itself out.

No police officer was fined, fired, or suspended. The mayor was reelected. Ramona Africa, the sole adult survivor of the attack and blaze, spent seven years in prison after conviction of rioting, conspiracy, assault—and for surviving. Philadelphia became the first American city to drop an incendiary device on its own citizens, shoot into a burning house, and let an entire street burn down. No automatic weapons were found in the rubble. Six dead adults and five children were.

No child left behind—alive.

ELEGY (excerpt)

    by Sonia Sanchez, Philadelphia poet

1.
philadelphia
a disguised southern city
squatting in the eastern pass of
colleges cathedrals and cowboys
philadelphia, a phalanx of parsons
and auctioneers
modern gladiators
erasing the delirium of death from their shields

2.
c'mon girl hurry on down to osage st
they're roasting in the fire
smell the dreadlocks and blk/skins
roasting in the fire.

c'mon newsmen and tvmen
hurryondown to osage st and
when you have chloroformed the city
and after you have stitched up your words
hurry on downtown for sanctuary
in taverns and corporations
and the blood is not yet dry

3.
how does one scream in thunder?

3
KIDS FOR SALE

Olney Avenue to Wyoming Avenue

I F you think growing up in an insecure, violent city under attack from without and within, by simpleton police chiefs and pyromaniac mayors and mad-dog media and manic-depressive standups and cuckolded uncles and the fat, unshaven newspaper dude down the corner doesn't take a mighty toll on your soul, you are not a Philadelphian. Corrosive and permanent damage is the prognosis. Many of us were nourished by a steady diet of civic shame and invective. The city's advertising slogan of the 1970s was "Philadelphia Is Not As Bad As Philadelphians Say It Is." Oh yes it was! A clever phrase, perhaps, an attempt to turn self-loathing inside out, it proved inaccurate and unconvincing, and no outsider wanted to visit a dog of a town whose mangy inhabitants were so scarred, so flea-bitten that they kicked themselves before you had the chance. Self-image? You want to know about self-image? Coming up, this Philadelphian was nourished by a steady diet of shame and invective. Philly was Taint. That's the notion I was reared on. Philadelphia as the Taint of America, taint being street lingo for the perineum—t'aint pussy, t'aint asshole, it's the taint. In the Northeast Corridor, t'aint New

York, t'aint Washington, it's Filthydelphia. The Taint. Not exactly Our Town, this taint, but something one heard, and sensed, throughout childhood. Taint. Trust me, growing up on the reeky patch of flesh between erogenous zones can twist a young mind like a pretzel.

To understand how ineradicable this stigma can be, consider this: between 1969 and 1972, twelve men walked on the moon. They were among the astronauts gathered in a room at NASA when a lecturer asked the assemblage one question: "What is the moon made of?" Everyone in the room, in unison, said green cheese. Even the men who had walked upon the lunar rock and soil. That's how deeply ingrained teachings go. Crater steep and crater wide. A depression on the brain's surface. You spend a lifetime unlearning such lessons, acquiring perspective, gaining distance, and sometimes 230,000 miles into space is not enough.

What's worse than firebombing your own citizens? Philadelphians knew that self-flagellation by conflagration was just a manifest expression of a deep disturbance. Everyone gave up on Philly, especially the indigenous people. Philadelphians latched on to and cultivated their image as vicious Cheez Whiz–dripping fans so rabid that an on-site criminal court was gaveled into session at every Eagles home game at Vet Stadium. Belligerence, chauvinism, parochialism. Reputation was reality and vice versa. Not that being a Philadelphian is a self-conscious act or a daily grind; it's neither a burden nor a source of pride until questioned or confronted. Philadelphianism is as natural as breathing or hating New York. New Yorkers are more aware of their New Yorkness and much more prone to frequent and foolish self-promotion, causing one to wonder if they mean it, or if putting up with all that New York nonsense—high rent, high buildings, high tensions, high ambitions, high neighbors—entitles them to transparently false bragging rights. They are surely clinically insecure, for they have no reason to be insecure. Philly has good reason to be insecure: New York.

Having New York a hundred miles to the north is like having a big brother in the upper bunk who composes short stories like Salinger, show tunes like Sondheim, and canvases like Jean Michel Basquiat, and then plays softball on weekends like Mickey Mantle and rushes home to cook Sunday dinner like Mama Leone. Fuggedaboutit. You live in a long cold shadow and always feel inferior. It ain't neurotic to feel inferior if you really are inferior, is it?

Having Washington a hundred miles to the south is a constant reminder that Philly used to be the capital of the country, used to be the shaper of national tastes and standards, used to be a city to be reckoned with.

This takes an incalcuable toll.

"I spent two years in Philadelphia," writes Dr. JAS at prisoners.com, a Web site run by prisoners for the benefit of the 100,000-plus prisoners in Pennsylvania. "I have to say that I had some of the worst experiences in my life in that city! Basically, my pessimistic outlook of the area was reaction to the sociology of the people. . . . I didn't meet a single person in Philadelphia that seemed normal to me.

"Most had very serious problems with their relationships, alcohol, illicit drugs, and bad behavior. I've traveled all over the world and I've dealt with various levels of society. Philadelphia is one horrible place to live and base your upbringing on. I feel sorry for those who will never understand how debilitated they are."

Approaching Olney Avenue, a bus and subway stop, a major street with pedestrian traffic, folks are ambling about, in no particular hurry, and no stores are crowded. There is a small-town feel to it all. Friendly. I stop at the Earl Scheib Paint and Body Shop for nostalgia's sake.

The manager's name is Vijay Chintaman. I ask him if the current price for a paint job is still $29.95.

"Oh, that was such a long time ago." Vijay laughs. He speaks with a Hindi accent. "The basic is now $229.95. Two coats and a one-year warranty against fading and peeling. The best deal is $499—you get three coats and a six-year warranty. Free estimates for bodywork. If you drop off your car in the morning, you can pick it up that evening."

Once again, I am not certain his accent is Hindi. I have no idea from what part of the world Vijay Chintaman hails.

"Guyana," he says before I can ask.

"Oh, Guyana," I say, as if I know where it is. I do not. All I know is that there are jungles in Guyana and I know that because Rev. Jim Jones set up his doomsday village in the jungle in Guyana and nine hundred people died when they drank arsenic-laced Kool-Aid one hot day in the name of loyalty and religion.

"Yes, Guyana," he says.

"I've been to Africa," I say, "but only Kenya and Uganda."

"I would like to visit Africa one day," says Vijay Chintaman. "You might be thinking of Ghana. That's in West Africa. Very large country. Guyana is very small, less than half a million people. In South America. Between Venezuela and Brazil."

"Well, your English is excellent," I say.

"English is the predominant language in Guyana," he says. His accent comes from his exposure to Portuguese, Hindi, Chinese, St. Lucian Creole French, Urdu, Arawak, Atorada, Berbice Creole Dutch, Carib, Macushi, Mapidian, Mawajana, Patamona, Pemon, Waiwai, Wapishana, Warao, and a patois or two.

Vijay Chintaman moved to America in 1978 and listened to Earl Scheib commercials on the radio his very first night here. He recites the ad copy verbatim: "I'll paint any car any color for $29.95. No ups! No extras!" The company has painted more than ten million cars over its sixty-eight years in business and still has over one hundred shops in the U.S. Vijay Chintaman was fascinated by the concept of someone painting your car. He was fascinated by the fact of cars. As of a decade ago, of the eight thousand kilometers of highway in Guyana, only six hundred were paved. Of the fifty airports, five were paved. Swamps and jungle, jungle and swamps. Cars are a different animal in Guyana.

"That's my truck," says Vijay, pointing to a new Infiniti SUV.

"Nice," I say.

"My wife had her car painted here, and my son too. My truck doesn't need it. May I take a look at your car?"

"I don't have a car."

"Oh," says Vijay. "Why not?"

"I am walking Broad Street," I say.

"Why are you doing that?" he asks.

"I don't know," I say.

Vijay doesn't quite understand the walking part any better than I do. He reaches under the desk and pulls out a special coupon that gets me half off the usual $399 for the 100 percent acrylic-urethane Euro-Paint© Lab Tested . . . Infrared Quartz Finish Dryer . . . Hand & Machine Sanding for Adhesion—with a 3 Year Limited Warranty.

As I leave, Vijay Chintaman asks me where I have come from.

"Why do you ask, because I have no car?"

"No, because you have no accent," says the Guyanan-American. "No Philadelphia accent."

What a charming thing to say. Many have tried but no one has really captured the whys and wherefores of the Philadelphia accent. Something about a stuffed nose and wide-open o's and t's turned into d's or jettisoned altogether. Like obscenity, you can hear it if you want to. Raised in a school with boys from all over America, and with twenty-five years in New York under my belt, I have lost much of my own Phillyffya accent, but on a good day, or a regressed day, I can torture vowels, convert t's into d's, and make whole syllables go missing with the best of them. Directions to a stranger might sound like this: "If yore comin from downashore, where the whodder is way too cold in the winner, ewe awdda come over the Wall Women Bridge, past where the Iggles play, and go shtraight through Glillilly. The Schoolkill Espressway is brutal, so ewe best keep a good addeetude. Anyways, take a tore down Broad and ewe'll find Senner Sydee right there unner Billy Penn's hat. Stop by and say hello to your favorite

mare and mayan, John Shtreet. Continue north past the Inkwire
Building, but avoid anything to do with Temple Als foopball program. It's like a friggin plegue hit Phillyffya and the all the Als caught
the avian flu."

"PRIVATE PROPERTY . . . WEAPONS ARE PROHIBITED . . . FOR
ADMISSION, APPLY AT THE FRONT DESK." The doors are locked
on the Broad Street side of this institution, so you have to go around
to the main entrance on Olney Avenue. A uniformed guard wants to
know if I have any questions. "Is this Girls' High or Gitmo?"

"Are you picking up your daughter?" he asks.

"No. I'd like to go the principal's office."

"Follow me," he says, and chaperones me to the principal's office.
The old school smells like all old schools and walking to the principal's office has a familiar unnerving feel. You have taken this walk before. Many times. The principal at my school paddled me so often I
took to wearing two and three pairs of underwear to school. Just in
case.

On the wall of this principal's office are posted the Top Ten Safety
Tips. Number 2 states: "Avoid wearing expensive trendy fashions to
and from school . . . Fila jackets, leather jackets with fringe sleeves, et
cetera." (Et cetera is spelled out.) Number 8 is: "AVOID BRINGING
LARGE SUMS OF MONEY TO SCHOOL" (you have to tell smart
girls this?). Number 10: "Students are not allowed to leave campus
during the school day . . . to purchase lunch or for any other reason."

(Too bad. A half block away, on Broad Street, is the Golden Krust
Bakery and Grill, where all Reggaefest Combos of Curried Goat or
Braised Oxtail come with rice, peas, and a Pepsi.) Whew. Glad I'm not
a kid anymore. The world has sure turned ugly, what with . . . wait a
minute . . . what am I talking about? I couldn't leave campus either.
Hell, I couldn't travel from one room to another without a pink pass
signed by a teacher or housemaster with the time, date, and reason
for travel. This is a picnic compared to my school, with its ten-foot-

high stone wall and the NAACP marching at the front gate and gangs of toughs waiting for us to hop the wall so they could hop us. Girard College. It pours out of me without warning, without much provocation. It's as if my filament is pure Girard and my skin porous. I have to focus on Girls' High now and the announcement for the "Daddy Daughter Dance." The what? "Dress to impress" says the poster. "Semi-formal . . . $40 a couple . . . deejay . . . driver's license ID required (for Daddies)." I ask a few girls if they will be attending the soiree. No way, they say, thoroughly creeped out by the idea of getting down with Daddy to a long Roots rap. One has similar difficulty imagining Dr. Freud attending a Saturday night ball at Vienna Girls' High and waltzing the night away with little Anna.

The thought gives new meaning to the ubiquitous signs around the school: "24-HOUR HOTLINE 215-299-SAFE."

I dial the number. It rings seven times. "School District Safeline," says the prerecorded message, and suggests I call 911 if there is a clear and present danger, that this line is for public school matters that require research or investigation, such as harassing, bullying, truancy. It turns out it is used more by teachers than students.

Arline Amaroso has seventeen years teaching experience and the patience of a stalking cat. South Philly born and bred, she will not be needing any hotlines. She learned her Italian at home, then on the streets, and eventually in Italy on a Fulbright Scholarship. She is teaching her advanced Italian class. The students chatter constantly, inanely, in English, a tiding of magpies. Ms. Amaroso teaches on. Of her eight students—whose Italian is unmelodic and halting at best—one is Asian, two African-American, three Caucasian, and two girls of mixed and indecipherable origin. One girl, with dark lustrous shoulder-length hair, is wearing a black bra that refuses to stay underneath a tight white muscle T-shirt. A detailed description of this girl, from head to toe, appears in my notes, scribbled across the blue lines, into the margins, as if by a pubescent boy or a dying man, inattentive to his own cursives, distracted by a hormonally charged girl whose underwear is under nothing. The school's dress code dictates white tops with black or khaki bottoms. The dress code is very relaxed. Suddenly, I am tapping Dr. Freud on the shoulder and asking him if I might have the next dance with his daughter.

"Shhhhhhhhh," says Ms. Amaroso, lifting a finger to her lips as one girl has finally gotten too loud and disruptive.

"*You* shush!" that girl yells back.

"*Quanto nella vostra famiglia?*" the teacher asks the student.

"*Cento,*" answers the impertinent one.

"*Quanto . . . nella . . . vostra . . . famiglia?*" Ms. Amaroso repeats slowly.

"*Cen . . . to,*" repeats the girl piu lento.

"*Cento* means a hundred," blares another student.

"I know that," snaps the ace student. "I got a big family, yo!"

"*Mamma mia,*" says the teacher.

Grapevines are stenciled above the blackboard like an Italian frieze. Irregular Italian verbs are conjugated on the board. The textbook is filled with splashy four-color photos to abet translations; photos of a kitchen (*la cucina*) and a camera (*una macchina fotografica*) and an Alfa Romeo (*Alfa Romeo*); photos of Kevin Costner and Sophia Loren and Woody Allen and Luciano Pavarotti. The school system could save money if it just passed around old *People* magazines it could lift from doctors' offices in Rome.

Two thirds of all students who take a foreign language in high school will forget nearly everything they learn and never use the language again. You take a young child, two or three years old, brain like a sponge, and she can learn two or three languages in the same span it takes the average American kid to learn one. No extra intelligence needed. It just happens. Without homework. Without memorizing irregular verbs. After three years old, humans lose a large capacity to hear and reproduce sound. Any country that starts language after elementary school is not serious about language. Why should we be? We are Americans. Everyone speaks American. It is the language of the

world. It is the language of the invading power. It is the language of
the Internet. When one of my sons was studying Buddhism at the
Kopan Monastery on a mountain in Nepal, I called him on the telephone. The monk who answered said, "Telephone bad—Internet
only," and hung up. In exchange for room and board and dharma lessons, my son was teaching the monks English. Before the Internet,
they had never cared about English.

Since Girls' High is a fast-track school, the students here are ahead
of the game: they are forgetting everything before they graduate.
They can barely order a good meal at a bad Italian restaurant.

It is a mild day, and the street and little park across from Albert
Einstein Medical Center are the most populated I've seen since starting out, people walking with purpose, people wearing green scrubs,
blue scrubs, colorful dashikis, black chadors, brown burkas, hijabs,
Iverson jerseys, Eagles caps, black boots, short skirts, butterfly tattoos, rainbow hair.

I am not going into Albert Einstein Medical Center for many reasons, chief among them that my father was pronounced dead in that
place after a heart attack after work one night after securing a mortgage on a new house on North 10th Street after returning from
World War II. Two children were left behind, sons aged three years
and six weeks respectively, and one wife, and she went to bed most
nights with a bottle of Scotch and the sad reality that things had not
worked out the way she had planned. It was not the first time, nor
the last.

My mother thought she was going to marry my father's brother,
Leon, before the attack on Pearl Harbor, which might as well have included the bombing of a certain woman in Philadelphia. Leon would
come a-courtin' from Baltimore on weekends, driving to West Philly
with at least one of his five brothers; there was a sister too, Molly. When
America joined the war, Leon and Morris signed up together. Another
brother was already in the European theater. When it was over, in 1945,
Morris, who had fought in France, Italy, and Africa, returned with some

medals, some shrapnel, the lingering effects of malaria, and the personal effects of his dead brother, Leon. Morris gave the letters, the uniform, and the bayonet of his dead brother to his dead brother's sweetheart. And then he fell in love with her. Or maybe he had been in love with her all along. My mother couldn't say no, even though her love was less certain. He was six foot three with a thin mustache and sly shy smile. He was tender and doting and went to business school in the day and worked at the Post Office on the graveyard shift, and came home and woke up his first son to play with him, and three years later, his second son too. My mother told me he was the kindest man she ever knew.

She also told me I killed him. Just like that. It was a few months after his death, even though I didn't know he was dead at the time, the funeral having been kept a secret from me and relatives feeding me fanciful and contradictory stories about his disappearance—he returned to the Army, he was on special duty for the Post Office, he went somewhere to do something. It's hard to explain death to a three-year-old, even if it means telling him a pack of lies instead and even if the three-year-old knows something has gone terribly wrong. And then one day, I was lying on my mother's bed as she was putting away freshly laundered clothing and I bugged her about the where-abouts of my father and she blew her cork and yelled, "He's dead! He's dead and you killed him!"

That's what I remember. How could I forget? I have tried. I have paid people to help me try. What she meant, what she told me years later, was that he was going to school by day and working at night and the pressure of having two children and a new mortgage and a princess wife was all too much for a man already weakened by war and malaria and the loss of two brothers. He was thirty-four.

At Duncannon Avenue, Our Lady of Hope Roman Catholic Church holds mass at 10:30 every Sunday in Spanish. Oh, to speak my second language. Aside from Puerto Ricans, who have a vibrant population in Philadelphia—the third largest in America—it took Latinos a long time to discover Philadelphia. The city's incredible shrinking population in the 1990s was not replenished by immigrants, legal or otherwise, almost all of whom preferred to settle elsewhere in the New World, places like Mississippi and North Carolina. Philadullphia was less than magnetic. It had all the dazzling downsides of urban life and none of the ups: no jobs, no hope, no dreams, wet, pipe, or American. At the end of the first year of the new millennium, 26,000 abandoned houses and 31,000 vacant lots were being used as makeshift trash dumps and shooting galleries and rodent refuges and lovers' lanes for desperate, carless couples. The official advertising pledge that "Philadelphia Loves You Back" would have been more effective had it read "Philly Watches Your Back." Homicides were up 20 percent. Tourism was down the tubes. Downadelphia seemed no better than Tijuana or Durango. There were virtually no Mexicans in Philly.

And then Efren Tellez strolled into town. He had left San Mateo Ozolco and paid a coyote to smuggle him into the U.S. New York City was too crowded with Latinos, none of them family, so he crossed the Jersey border, sans coyote, and ventured into Philadelphia. He wandered around, alone, despondent, until he passed a sign in a Center City window that said "Comida Mexicana." Unsure if he should ask for food or a job or directions home, he walked in and was hired as a dishwasher before he could say too much. Philly had been waiting for him. He sent word back to San Mateo that a virgin territory needed men who knew their way around the kitchen. *La sincronización era perfecta.* The Philly restaurant renaissance was about to happen, so Tellez's family and friends started to trickle into town, illicit and energetic, and word spread and soon a stream developed, and then the deluge. The young men of San Mateo Ozolco turned Philadelphia into an alimentary pilgrimage.

Of a village of maybe four thousand, a full third can be found in Philadelphia working as busboys, dishwashers, cooks, waiters. They live crammed into apartments, mostly in South Philly, and they work fifty to sixty hours a week, and bring home, on average, $400.

The son of Efren Tellez, the godfather of Mexadelphia, now works the line in a restaurant and plays on the soccer team called Aguilas; the eagle on the Mexican flag is the symbol of both home and adopted home. Mexadelphia's population has nearly tripled from the start of the decade and estimates now range from 7,500 to 12,000. Estimates are all you'll ever get. Most Mexadelphians happily fly under the radar.

Before Mexicans, most illegals in Philly were Italians and Irish and Chinese, relatives from the Old Country who came for a visit and never left. Some learned English, some didn't. Some became citizens, some didn't. No harm, no foul. They blended into the environment. The Philadelphia ethos is so pungent, so potent that your Mexican/Chinese great-grandchildren will be eating cheesesteaks with jalapeño peppers and rice.

Lindley, Ruscomb, Rockland. These streets trigger endorphins. This is my old neighborhood, Logan. I shot pool at Willie Mosconi's (gone) and saw movies at the Broad (gone) and worked with my mother at Perfect Photo (gone) and was born in a house four blocks away on 10th Street (gone—the house and the street).

Luckily, I saw the house years ago and for the last time. The metal glider was no longer on the front porch and I couldn't bring myself to impose upon the current residents to see the backyard where my brother blew up birds with improvised explosive devices or rummage through the basement where my father stored his golf clubs. I fear that basement is now permanently flooded. According to news reports, all the houses on my old block had been built on a stream that had been filled in in 1910 and it took until the 1980s for the houses to "settle," which is a risible euphemism for "fall down." The fills went forty-five feet deep. So did the houses. It took a long time to find out, but the landfills didn't work out the way the engineers had planned. Gone.

Other streets have held up better. Some are still totally empty, devoid of structures, like a stretch in Baghdad, bombed out, wondering what comes next. And then there are blocks that are the urban equivalents of an unprosperous Jersey strip mall. I walk up and down Broad, between Loudon and Rockland Streets, in a daze, taking in all the stores, like Ed Ruscha's *Every Building on the Sunset Strip,* only I jot down the names instead of taking their photos. On the west side of Broad, you have the OK Laundromat, Tony's Palace Pizza, Micro or Kinky Hair Braiding, Chiropractic Center, Sunny's Broad Deli, MuKund Patel Family Dentist, KWA 4830, Personal Touch Nail Salon, Al-Furqan Bookstore and Bazaar Islamic Center, Wyoming Medical Center, Grace's Essence of Beauty, African Braiding, Personal Touch PreSchool Annex, Lee's Market, Logan Child Care, and Circles Bar.

On the east side of Broad, from Loudon to Rockland, you have the Community Center, Phantasy Transportation, King of Rims, Aftermath Automotive Technology, Local 837 (in a theater), Church of Faith Hope & Love, Olney Logan Medical Center, Quality Real Estate, Broad Street African Hair Braiding, Diamond Nail Salon, Padilla's Italian and Hispanic Restaurant, Diamond Total Glamor, Dentists Felice Hom-Au and Raymond Au, Dollar Heaven—Milk, Eggs, Balloons, Keys, Amy's African Hair Braiding, Cho Viet Hai Oriental Grocery Store, Total Risk Management Inc., and the Broad and Rockland Beer Distributor.

With all those establishments, you would expect a street teeming with consumers. You would be wrong. That was the plan. It was wrong.

Broad and Wyoming has a Baptist church, a Wendy's, a Burger King, and a Dunkin' Donuts. I have to sit down for a moment and collect my thoughts. I want to say Broad and Wyoming is my grits, my gravy, my morning tea, except I am drinking coffee and eating a donut. Everyone here is drinking coffee and eating donuts. But no one is smoking. I miss smoking. I miss secondhand smoke. Maybe America got fat when it stopped smoking. Ta-ta Marlboros, hello Starbucks. Coffee helped kick the nicotine habit because it provided a little risk, gave you a minor buzz, and there was something to do with your mouth and hands when talking to a friend or driving a car. Fortunate folks stopped right there. But caffeine turned out to be a gateway drug—everyone was rushing around with a cup of joe in their hand but feeling tired all the time and needing something harder, longer lasting, more damaging. They needed food.

As smoking decreased, obesity increased. In the mid-1980s, 18 percent of America was overweight. Today, it's 64 percent. The average adult has gained ten pounds in the past ten years. At this rate, every third grown-up will explode in the year 2057. Could it be that smoking was actually healthier?

According to the Centers for Disease Control, the following ailments are associated with being overweight: depression, diabetes, alcoholism, hypertension, gallstones, liver disease, gout, sleep apnea, arthritis, angina, stroke, hernias, blood clots, urinary infections, skin ulcers, and, last but not least, six types of cancer. Treating these conditions adds $100 billion a year to health care costs (half by government) and that surpasses the costs generated by smoking.

I need a cigarette.

I don't smoke. Used to. Started as a teenager. Smoked in front of my mother too. What could she say, her being a Pall Mall fiend and all. I was smoking right over there, at the corner of Broad and Wyoming, during the summer of 1962 when I first met Angie Lombino's boyfriend. It was a great day.

An old Oldsmobile stopped at the curb and a muscular Italian guy clad in an Italian muscle shirt jumped out of his car and rushed up to me and hit me in the face with a well-aimed roundhouse right. I dropped my cigarette.

"If you talk to Angie again," he said, "I'll kill you."

As he drove away, I caught a glimpse of Angie Lombino riding shotgun.

Two thoughts struck me immediately after his fist: how little the punch hurt and how much Angie Lombino must like me. It was a wildly exhilarating moment. Angie Lombino looked great, by the way, as she always did.

Angie Lombino was a neighborhood girl with so much jet black hair she didn't know what to do with it all. Some days it was up and swirled around, and other days it hung down her back like stygian ivy. She was petite with a perfectly rounded behind, adorable in the way only shy Italian girls could be, and you knew she would be a generous lover, passionate and polite at the same time, like a good Catholic girl who gets on *American Bandstand* because she looks so sweet and then dances up a callipygian storm. To say I had a serious crush on Angie Lombino would be an understatement. I would take a punch for her. And smile. We attended different schools, and ran in different circles, and she was so shy and scared she never talked to me again, except to warn me about her boyfriend and look around nervously and keep walking.

I forgot to mention that when Angie Lombino's boyfriend landed his roundhouse right to my cheek, I was standing between my mother and little brother. We were waiting for the C bus to go downtown to see *Lawrence of Arabia,* a movie someone should have forced George W. Bush to watch before his Iraq debacle. Angie Lombino's boyfriend was confined to a one-punch fight, in part because my mother shrieked and attacked him with flailing fists when she realized what was taking place. I have no idea what his plan was, but he left the scene abruptly. It was one of the few times I remember my mother protecting me, coming to my rescue without strings, without regard for herself, without an agenda. Pure visceral motherhood. Or so I would like to think. What a day. Angie. Mom. Lawrence. And the knowledge that I did not have a glass jaw.

4

NO SIGNS OF INDIANS

Wingohocking Street to Elser Street

WINGOHOCKING is my favorite street name, to say, to spell—the first O of Wingohocking is missing on this street sign. Chief Wingohocking is turning over in his sacred burial site (if there are any left in Philadelphia). Even the street sign makers do him wrong. Wingohocking wound up with a namesake street because of the deal he made with James Logan, who, at twenty-seven, ran the colony whenever his friend, William Penn, the First Immigrant, returned to England. (Which was often, and for prolonged periods.) Chief Wingohocking wanted to exchange names with James Logan as an act of mutual respect. Logan declined, but promised to name the lovely stream winding through his estate for the chief.

Wingohocking Creek now flows beneath Belfield Avenue, long buried in the city sewer system. Is this what we have done to our Indian history?

The Leni Lenape ("true people") became the Delaware and were forced west. So diplomatic were the Leni Lenape that they were called in by other tribes to settle disputes. When Thomas Jefferson called

William Penn "the greatest law-giver the world has produced," he was using Penn's compact with the Indians—the Plan of Union—as a template for the U.S. Constitution; almost no credit was given to Penn's negotiating partners, the Leni Lenape, who knew a few things about governing a nation from a thousand years of experience.

The Mingoes were here, and the Wyandots and the Nanticoke, but there are scant signs of their existence. Words like Schuylkill (meaning hidden river) and Wissahickon (meaning yellow-colored creek) have survived in the form of rivers, but the Leni Lenape to current ears sound more like a name for an Italian-American slacker in a screenplay than a noble tribe: "Yo, Lenny, Lenny Lenapi, you sleep too much! Get a freakin' job!"

Estimates guess that four thousand Native Americans currently live in the Philadelphia area. You wonder what they call this splendid Indian-summer day, since that label is but a slur; anything the colonists considered counterfeit was described as Indian, like Indian corn when you didn't know what was hidden by the husk. An Indian summer was a false summer, warmth in October or November that was offered and taken back, an illusion, a bad time for planting, another Indian trick.

The Leni Lenape, armed with bows and arrows, must have loved Hunting Park, as deer, rabbit, elk, fox, and ducks were plentiful. Now you find Domino's Pizza and New Orleans Chicken at Hunting Park Avenue and Broad Street. The area is decrepit. While imagining what a New Orleans chicken might look like, or sound like, a sign on the porch of a row home grabs your eye:

VIVERO LIVESTOCK & POULTRY—CHICKENS, DUCKS, RABBITS, TURKEYS, LAMBS, GOAT, COW and MORE.

More? How much more can there be? I knock on the front door. A man explains that the animals are around the corner, on Lycoming, a half block west of Broad. Even though the few paces west violate my own rules for the Long March, this I have to see.

From the outside, it looks like an old-time butcher shop, with the name ALBARAKA VIVERO stenciled on the front window. Albaraka is "The Blessed" in Arabic, and Vivero is "breeding ground" in Spanish. You think you'll find an actual melting pot inside. What you find in what used to be a garage are animals—white turkeys, guinea hens, pigeons, and rabbits—crammed into rectangular wooden crates piled as high as a horse's eye.

A thin, Semitic man tells me if I choose something now, he can deliver it after six this evening. Or tomorrow morning. There are only two delivery times—the days are reserved for slaughtering in that room over there, the one with the large door and small, splattered window.

"Is this halal?" I inquire.

"What is halal?" he inquires.

"A method of killing, of draining the blood, of—"

"Yes, yes, yes. It's halal. Halal."

"Local game?" I ask.

"Virginia, New Jersey, Pennsylvania."

Signs, pamphlets, handouts are all printed in English and Spanish. Patos, pavos, palomas, conejos, ovejas, vaca. Ducks, turkeys, pigeons, rabbits, sheep, cow. The birds and rabbits, you have to buy the whole creature—black roosters are $12 apiece, quails are $2, red broilers go for $1.50 per pound. From 8 A.M. to 7 P.M., seven days a week, you could be in any number of Third World countries, excited by the freshness, repulsed by the rawness. I am reminded of the kosher butcher of my childhood, less than a mile from this spot, sawdust on the floor, blood on the aprons, chickens and turkeys hanging in the window. How different is this?

"You want to see the larger animals?" I am asked.

"What larger animals?" I ask.

"We sell their parts by the pound," he says. "Vendemos carne por libra."

"What larger animals?" I ask again.

"Come with me," he says and waves his hand delicately. A short walk ends when he opens the door of a miniature barn, where goats and sheep and cows, small cows, baby cows, comprise a peaceable kingdom. Or an asylum for the shell-shocked and despondent. You feel your guts churning. This is death row, with no possibility of a last-minute call from the governor. Most of the animals are reclining on hay. There must be twenty sheep and fifteen goats and a half dozen calves, all in the same pen. This is no petting zoo. Though large floor fans are blowing, the urban abattoir is very hot and smelly. Your stomach reacts badly. You want to leave.

Now back in the first room, the rabbits stick in your craw. Black and brown and fat and dormant, they appear dead already—cooped up behind wooden bars, overcrowded, waiting for termination, praying to meet the Great White Rabbit. You wish they could rub their own legs for luck.

"You want a rabbit?" he asks in his Arabic/Latino accent. "What is you look for?"

A Jimmy Hoffa line pops to mind in pure comic defense, but is never uttered. Rampaging stomach acids prevent any chitchat. Salaam aleichem.

Outside, in the gloriously polluted city air, you take deep breaths to make certain you are not experiencing some Kafkaesque flashback hallucinogenic moment, and then you turn into a rat. You call the city authorities: how can this be legal? You are connected to Animal Care, then Adopted Pets, then EPA, then Robin Hood Dell, then Food Inspectors, and finally someone who knows about this place, has inspected this place, and says it's totally legit since they rezoned one building as a wholesale slaughterhouse and the adjacent building as a retail outlet. Call interruption interrupts. It's my brother, the Santa Monica vegetarian. I thank the inspector and press a button.

"Did you call me earlier?" my brother asks.

"I did."

"Are you really walking Broad Street?" he asks.

"Are you still sour on the cemetery plots?" I ask.

"So it wasn't a dream," he sighs.

"I have another idea, a new business for you."

"Why are you walking around Philly?"

"I'm on the road to find out," I say.

"Cat Stevens. Academy of Music. Nineteen seventy. Panama Red. Great concert. Great dope."

"Funny you should mention that," I say.

"Your new business involves Cat Stevens?"

"More like Hassan Stevens," I say.

"Is that Cat's new name?"

"No, that's the new business. halal fast food."

"I'll bite. What's that?" he asks.

"It's sort of like kosher, only for Muslims."

"Are you being held hostage, brother?"

"No. This is a great idea. Healthy food for the religious, the hip, and the antiwar crowd."

"I get it. A Blue State Special."

"I'm serious," I say. "And I know an East Coast distributor."

"Who wants to think about Iraq when eating a lamb chop?"

"Did you eat Vietnamese food before Vietnam?" I ask.

"What?"

"That's how it works," I say. "We invade a country, tear it to shreds, then love their food when they move here."

"Iraq, Iran, Iruin."

"Who ate kimchi before the Korean Conflict?" I ask.

"Koreans?"

"Exactly."

"I don't see a lot of Cambodian restaurants," he says.

"We never bombed Cambodia."

"We did so," he says.

"Not on the record. It only counts if it's on the record. Iraq is on the record, and someone's going to cash in on this healthy kosher/

Muslim fast food craze and I thought it could be you is all. Aren't there a lot of rich Arabs in Hollywood?"

"Can I call the place Abu Grub?"

"Jesus. You think that's a good idea?" I ask.

"You think starting another restaurant is a good idea?"

After attending the Jack Kerouac School of Disembodied Poetry, my brother opened an organic health food restaurant in Boulder. He made the world's oldest business error by hiring two relatives, two brilliant cousins; one, the family genius who invented multimedia, was the maître d' who berated the hungry hippies for their slouching posture and inelegant attire; the other was the family scientist, who came straight from a Catskills commune with Swami Satchinanda or Guru Maharaj Ji, and who, as head chef at Yarrowstalks, was known far and wide, if not for long, for chasing the waitress, his girlfriend, across the dining room and throwing dishes at her. He called them his "Black-and-Blue Plate Specials." The eatery, and the girlfriend, lasted six months.

You walk faster now, amped by memory and activity and the traffic, both foot and vehicular. In fact, as you pass Kerbaugh Street and then Elser, without warning, you enter some automotive haven, two odd blocks filled with Enterprise Rental, Bartos Auto Sales, AutoZone Auto Parts, Mike's Custom Aftermarket Installation Specialist, and a lot with old BMWs, gussied up with the name BMUC, or Bavarian Motors Used Cars. There are quite a few grease monkeys leaning into and sliding under cars with their hoods up. Most of them are smoking. The grease monkeys that is. Philadelphians love their cars. City dwellers don't need a car the way folks do in Austin or Miami, but Philadelphians are afraid of the subway, are bored by buses, find trolleys quaint, and wouldn't think of taking a taxi, when they are not on strike.

Taxis are expensive and are often jalopies. Some have seat belts that work, some don't. You may enter a cab one day, loaded down with

Christmas gifts, tell the driver your destination, and he will swivel around and say, "Close enough to walk. Get out, please." You will be stunned. The driver will stare at you. You will realize he hails from a country where carrying nicely wrapped packages twelve blocks in the middle of the day does not seem like a daunting physical or emotional task, so you will exit the cab and walk to your destination, powered by fumes.

5

No Child's Behind Left Behind

Erie Avenue to Susquehanna Avenue

THE sign at McDonald's at Broad and Erie claims 99 billion burgers sold. One more billion and it will hit 100 billion burgers. That would be 1 with 11 zeroes. There have been, since the beginning of time, 100 billion humans on planet earth. Most of them spent their between-meal time searching for their next meal. Today, 50 million people eat at McDonald's daily. Philadelphia has forty-seven McDonald's franchises. Seven are on Broad Street. Philadelphia has ranked in the top four fattest cities four times since 2000, meaning Philadelphia fatties finish higher in their league than the Phillies or Sixers or Flyers do in theirs. Obesity is not restricted to professionals or adults. Ten-year-olds now suffer what used to be called adult onset diabetes. This stunning development is due to kiddie obesity. The percentage of little league fatties in Philly has tripled since 1980.

No child's behind left behind.

If the trends continue, if my calculations are correct, the year 2047 will witness the perfect storm for Fattydelphia. Except for the infirm and the immigrants (if these groups are still permitted visas), 90 percent of the locals will be morbidly obese and McDonald's burger sales will hit 100 zeroes, or a googol. To celebrate, McDonald's will merge with Google and give away mini-computers with all Surf 'N' Turf Meals so the kiddies can surf the Net and wolf down burgers and no one will ever move faster than a turtle except professional athletes who will be paid to do all the running and jumping for the morbidly obese as they watch the athletes on itsy-bitsy screens given away free by McGoogle's.

In the meantime, hanging from a railroad overpass above Tioga Street is a red and white banner: TEMPLE UNIVERSITY—1¾ MILES AHEAD. This info is more for your central nervous system than your cardiological concerns, as you are entering the dark heart of North Philly, Desolation Row. The promise of Temple University, the oasis in this dilapidated desert, is meant to tranquilize. Temple won't let you get hurt. Temple can't afford it. Nor can the city. For if Broad Street is the spine of the metropolis, then Temple is the marrow, producing enough red and white cells to keep the urban blight at life-support levels. The Temple complex attracts 100,000 worker bees to B. Street every day, students and teachers and doctors and patients and clerks and guards and indigents and topers and shoppers. Undergrad and grad, intern and resident. A dental school here, a law school there. Temple Hospital down the road. Even in these days of neglect, good sense (and good business) dictates that the Temple Mile, from Tioga to Cecil B. Moore Avenue, must remain relatively safe and sound. Passable. So block after block, six-foot vermilion gonfalons with white Ts wave from light stanchions like ubiquitous hexes.

And the number of robberies in Philly has gone down every year since 2000. And assaults and thefts and burglaries. Rapes remain at one thousand a year. Only murders are increasing. Your money or your life is no longer a question. Drugs are not the driving force of crime. You can't buy esteem on the street and snort it or shoot it or smoke it. Respect is harder to come across than crack.

A siren from a speeding police car pierces the day. No one pays attention. To the police or me. I walk on. Neither brazen nor kowtowing, making apposite eye contact, I feel no menace. The vacant eyes that pass me by match the empty houses. Neither squalor nor the struggle against it can undo this implausibly relaxed mood. I am not unaware of the hazards—like students at Girls' High, I don't carry much money and I don't wear a leather jacket with fringe. I keep waiting for something. Anything. I suddenly want to call this part of the city, affectionately, ironically, NoBro, making the other side of City Hall SoBro. No one will go for it.

A benighted Broad Street, I surmise, must become the hellhole of its reputation. Is it possible that twenty-some years in New York have reduced Philadelphia, in my mind, to a minor-league crime scene? Broad Street likes being walked, digs the hustle and flow, and I have to force myself to remember that these are the mean streets I was warned about by family, friends, police records, and bloggers.

VirtualTourist.com has something called Warnings or Dangers. This posting by feline01 is typical: "There are some really bad neighborhoods in Philly for tourists. Avoid Broad Street near Temple University if possible and South Philly can be a bit rough depending exactly where you are. If you feel a bit nervous in a neighborhood, listen to that inner voice and get out quickly."

Is it possible that feline01 has read the introduction to the Philadelphia City Planning Commission's *Blight Certification*? "This report presents an evaluation of blight . . . in two areas spanning a relatively large portion of Upper North Philadelphia, Allegheny West and Tioga . . . previously certified as blighted in 1970 when the Tioga Redevelopment Area was established. Therefore, blight is being 're-certified' to make the information more current and up-to-date."

Still blighted after all these years. Even the word "blight" is from another era, from three decades ago, from a time when Urban Blight was a polite way of calling a slum a slum.

The 2003 report continues:

Key evidence [for blight] includes the following:

the presence of 1,003 vacant structures

the presence of 590 vacant lots (strewn with trash)

the presence of 4,228 properties with housing code violations

the presence of 588 buildings officially designated as "dangerous"

the presence of 2,973 vacant housing units (17 percent)

the presence of 4,228 properties in violation of the City
Housing Code

Census Property Values show a median value of $29,649 compared to the City's median value of $59,700 (2000 Census).

Therefore, property values in this area are approximately half of the City median.

The report concludes that once again, whereas and therefore, so be it decreed, indubitably and officially, much of North Philadelphia is indeed unpardonably blighted, and the city has just about given up trying to fix it, and despite a feeling of revival in Philadelphia in general, North Philly is fucked beyond hope, so walk around at your own peril and don't tell us we didn't warn you.

Blight on, baby. Keep your eyes open and your mouth shut. Every once in a while, someone or something will attract your attention, and you will want to get off the beaten path and venture down a side street. Resist the temptation. Stray from the straight and narrow, one block or ten, east or west, and the streets become alleys, looks grow furtive, you stand out like the sore white thumb you are, easily spotted, tagged, surveilled. You are suddenly in Morocco or Tikrit, the South Bronx or Corleone. The hood rules. And there are hoods within hoods, like Russian nesting dolls, like Chinese boxes, like Iraqi territories.

Clearly, you are in someone else's neighborhood, and it ain't Mister Rogers's. Self-appointed sentinels are on patrol for any foreigner who may be a cop, a thief, a bill collector, a real estate vulture, a drug dealer, a drug user, a cuckolder wooing someone's daughter or sister or brother or mother, or a freaky familial combo package. Trespassers beware. They are unforgiven. Stick to Broad Street, the longest straight green zone in America.

Broad Street is what the indigenous population gives you, neutral turf, a free passage, and you are shielded by that unwritten law, as well as the steady traffic, foot and wheel. Getting off the beaten path may get you beaten. In one way or another. Broad Street belongs to the daylight walker because the walker is just passing through, on his way to elsewhere, to school, to the hospital, to work, to a check-cashing joint, to McDonald's.

At Broad and Allegheny, McDonald's has a McPlayground. It is the first outdoor area designated for children you have seen. It's all primary colors and plastic, sliding boards and monkey bars. The area is devoid of kids; one teenager hangs out next to the Day-Glo castle with his boom box blaring. Last year, McDonald's started its "product placement rewards," paying any hip-hopper who mentions "Big Mac" in his music $5 per mention per artist per radio airplay. When you have thirty thousand restaurants, you have to plug away.

Gotta buy the bards, gotta stack the cards, Big M to the izzA, C to the Izz-D, eezy on the cheezy, no big schlamazzle.

Inside, the burger business is brisk. The frying fat attracts like urban nectar. What chance does a kid have? No better than a tree in a rain forest. For every pound of beef consumed, 220 square feet of rain forest have been destroyed. Every year, the planet loses 40 million acres of rain forest and Americans gain about that much in weight.

"Welcome to McDonald's. May I help you?"

"A Diet Coke, please."

"Would you like some fries today?" asks the man.

"What do you think of all these kids eating all this junk?"

"They like it," he says.

"You think it's good for them?" I ask.

"Will that be all today?"

"This is a very depressing place," I say.

"Yo, the best children's hospital in America has a Mickey D's. Don't be trippin' on me. That be a large Coke?"

"Medium. What hospital? Diet."

"The Children's Hospital."

I call Ms. Peggy Flynn, director of media relations at the Children's Hospital of Philadelphia.

"How can I help you?" asks Ms. Peggy Flynn.

"I'd like to ask a question about McDonald's," I say.

"I'll try to help you," says Ms. Peggy Flynn.

"Have there ever been internal debates about the wisdom of promoting fast food at a preeminent children's hospital?"

"I'll have to do some research on that," she says.

"Okay," I say.

"Give me a week or two," she says.

"A week or two?" I ask.

"Yes, a week or two," she says.

The Children's Hospital of Philadelphia was voted the best pediatrics facility in the country in a survey of board-certified physicians by *U.S. News & World Report*. When Ms. Peggy Flynn does not call back after one week or two, I call her.

"How did you know?" she wants to know.

"How did I know what?" I want to know.

"About the internal rumbling concerning McDonald's."

"I didn't know," I say.

"You knew. How did you know?"

"I was just curious. It seems like a natural question, the wisdom of serving fast food to sick children."

"I'll have to get back to you on that."

"On what?"

"The wisdom of whatever you said. Do you want written material or an interview with someone?"

"Both would be nice, Peggy."

"I'm just figuring out the best way to serve you."

"That sounds more like Burger King than McDonald's."

"Why are you doing this?" asks Ms. Flynn.

"That was an attempt at humor, Peggy."

"Oh," says Ms. Peggy Flynn.

A week later, Ms. Flynn calls to arrange an interview with Mr. Gavin Kerr, chief operating officer of the hospital.

"He can do it this week," she says, "or at the end of the month when the negotiations with McDonald's will be concluded."

"Negotiations?"

"With McDonald's," says Ms. Peggy Flynn.

"Negotiations about what?"

"Their lease is up."

"Is the hospital going to renew their lease?" I ask.

"I cannot delve into that," says Ms. Peggy Flynn.

"I understand, Peggy. As for the interview, the sooner the better."

The day before the interview, I get a call from Ms. Peggy Flynn. Mr. Gavin Kerr will speak to me at 3 P.M. the following day. If for any reason I will be unavailable at that time, I should call and let that be known.

Gavin Kerr is a mild-mannered, well-modulated gentleman of rectitude, even if he insists on referring to his hospital as CHOP. It is an unfortunate acronym. He has been the COO of CHOP for a year and half. McDonald's has been there for thirty years. Mr. Kerr is well aware of the contradiction inherent in a health-giver trading in fast food. The negotiations with McDonald's, he says, are not only about the length of the lease or the rent hike, but also about the literature CHOP wants to make available to Mickey D's customers. Mr. Kerr calls it a great opportunity to educate the public and guide them to better nutritional decisions.

"We have some of the sickest kids in the country, in the world for that matter, coming to CHOP. They are invariably in crisis. A hospital can be scary, so we try to provide a comfortable, safe place. My son had cancer four years ago, so as a father I was here a lot. My son didn't like needles, but I could say to him, 'If you do this, we'll go get a chocolate milk shake at McDonald's.' It may not be the most nutritious food, but when you're on chemo, calories are critical. It may be the only thing some of these kids can eat. We can use McDonald's as motivation."

How can anyone argue with the parent of a cancer kid? One can but listen and marvel at the smart hirings at CHOP.

"We like having an influence on food intake—take the opportunity to educate at every turn. A nutritionist works with every family where nutrition or diet is part of the medical plan. We want to be able to guide the families. In the end, it's mainly the families of the sick kids and the employees who use McDonald's. It's open twenty-four hours. The cafeteria is only open from 6 A.M. to 8 P.M."

As delicately as possible, I suggest there may be ways around McDonald's if the COO of CHOP were so inclined—Mickey D's is not the only purveyor of chocolate shakes. Just seeing a McDonald's at a respected health care center might do more harm than good, over the long haul. How can a parent ever tell a recovered cancer patient, or diabetic, or a brother or sister of the sick kid, that McDonald's ought to be avoided when it's right there at the best kids' hospital in the world for the sickest kids in the world? As for the hours, any cafeteria could stay open if that were a requirement; and if it were the only eatery on the premises, it would do just fine. What if, God forbid, the food outlet at the hospital did not turn a profit?

In the background, I can hear Ms. Peggy Flynn's muffled voice saying things like, "I still don't know why he's asking all these questions."

"McDonald's is not evil," states Kerr flatly, undefensively. "If I ate at an expensive steak house every day for a week, that would be unhealthy as well."

Check please. That's a mockery of logic, and Mr. Kerr ought to know it. No one is talking about gluttony or gout, rather a tacit approbation of junk food, the miseducation of children, the setting of poor examples. Listen to Alice Waters, food connoisseur and creator of the organic lunch program in Berkeley: "Not only are our children eating this unhealthy food, they're digesting the values that go with it: the idea that food has to be fast, cheap, and easy; that abundance is permanent and effortless; that it doesn't matter where food actually comes from. . . . The children we're raising now will probably die younger than their parents of diseases that are largely preventable by diet and exercise."

There is no reason under the sun for a world-class children's hospital to be a purveyor of any McMuckamuck.

You can see William Penn through the pollution or the mist. Even from this distance, about three miles away, from 3000 North Broad, the Old Quaker looms over Philly like a miniature Christ the Redeemer over Rio. At thirty-seven feet tall, Penn is the tallest statue on any building in the world; his hat is twenty-three feet around, his nose is eighteen inches long (and not from lying.) Pigeons no longer make him their home: Penn was made pigeon poop–proof after thirty-seven tons of bird droppings were removed in 1993. He stands atop the largest municipal building in the nation—550 feet high. Penn's five-foot left hand points northeast, to the village of Shackamaxon, where he signed a monumental treaty with the Indians in 1682. Philadelphia was purchased that day for £1,200. The peace section of the compact was broken as soon as Penn was out of sight. It wasn't his lie. The Leni Lenape were forced into New Jersey, then west to Ohio, Missouri, and finally Oklahoma. And Canada.

Another famous statue, less immobile, is the nine-foot hunk of bronze that used to sit atop the art museum steps until its propinquity to bona fide art became too hilarious, too painful to bear, and it was moved to the Spectrum, a sports arena in South Philly. Rocky is, needless to say, the fictional, bighearted, pea-brained, semiverbal underdog portrayed by a New Yorker who lives in Los Angeles and prefers polo to the sweet science. Rocky, he gets a statue. Joe Frazier, he gets a dark tiny gym at Broad and Indiana.

Frazier's gym is on the ground floor. The door is open, and if it gets stuck on occasion, a sign says push harder or ring the bell. Joe lives upstairs. You walk right in, around midday. "Hello, anybody home?" No one answers, not even the older man sitting on the far side of the ring, white-haired head down, reading through the glasses on the end of his nose, unaware he is not alone. Strands of sunlight hang across the room dominated by a boxing ring, with a handful of heavy bags and speed bags hanging, leaving barely enough space to shadowbox, or jump rope while facing a wall filled with Joe Frazier paintings, Joe Frazier posters, Joe Frazier publicity stills, Joe Frazier photographs and a brief bio, writ large, right there on the wall. As positive and uplifting as the collage tries to be, melancholy is the effect. Joe Frazier worked in a slaughterhouse during his teen years. Joe Frazier practiced his jabs and hooks on sides of beef. Joe Frazier ran through the streets of Philadelphia. Sound familiar? Sound like a certain movie character? Sylvester Stallone spun Joe Frazier yarns into white gold.

We tend to forget that Frazier was an Olympic gold medalist. And his heavyweight record was 32-4-1. And he lost only to George Foreman and Muhammad Ali. (He maintains he never lost to Ali, only to the judges and refs.) He is a beloved and bejeweled local hero. So how come sadnesses accompany him like an entourage? Not chronicled on the wall are Smokin' Joe's post-career arrests for domestic violence, for drunk driving, for packing a .357 Magnum without a license, for losing millions in failed business ventures. Not chronicled are the taunts and degradations inflicted by Muhammad Ali that fueled the public perception of Smokin' Joe as a Tom, a gorilla, a tongue-tied palooka, a punch-drunk establishment dupe. Not chronicled is the moment in 1996 when Smokin' Joe, after watching Ali shakily light the Olympic fire in Atlanta, said he would like to throw Ali into that fire. Even though your left brain knows Smokin' Joe was a world champeen and is renowned to this day, he still qualifies as another patsy in the long line of tragic Philadelphia patsies in your right brain: Meldrick Taylor. Jimmy Young. Gypsy Joe Harris. Tyrone Everett. Hard drugs and loves gone wrong and fortunes squandered and lives lost too soon.

You walk around the dingy gym with the random lockers and headgear. You take notes. You feel queasy. This is not how Joe Frazier planned it, how he envisioned his golden years. The real deal is getting a raw deal. You think about saying goodbye to the old man with the reading glasses, maybe ask him how Smokin' Joe is doing. You don't know if the man is reading or napping. You don't want to disturb him.

The light of day hurts your eyes. The visit didn't turn out how you planned it. You want to ring the bell for the apartment above the gym, the one-bedroom flat where Joe Frazier lives. You don't. You can't. You wish you were selling furniture.

At the corner of Broad and Indiana, in front of a small shopping mall, I pass a chubby black dude hiding behind sunglasses and a black baseball cap.

"Socks," he says. "Six pair for five dollars."

I'm set with socks, so I just walk on by. Halfway down the block, I think maybe it's not socks he's selling, maybe that's a euphemism, a street code for some other contraband, something more imaginative, perhaps imported. What the hell.

"Socks?" I ask, eyebrow raised steeply.

"Socks," says the man.

"Where are your socks from?"

"Heaven," says the vendor.

"You got socks from heaven?"

"Direct from heaven," he says.

"How did they get to you?"

"I am blessed, brother, blessed."

And I am flummoxed. Is he really dealing socks on the street? I see a box of them, white, cotton, wrapped in plastic. Socks?

"How much are the socks?" I ask.

"Six pair, five dollars."

"How much do these blessings bring you each day?"

"Oh, you wanna concentrate on the money aspect," he says.

"Do you make a living selling socks on Broad Street?"

"People don't need socks," he says. "People need a spiritual encounter. A psychological encounter. Something to lift them up. You have to see beyond what is seeable. You read Deepak Chopra, right?"

"Some," I say, lying.

"In *Ageless Body, Timeless Mind*, he deals with quantum physics and how the physical is false. The masters all know that. Buddha, Jesus, Gandhi, Kahlil Gibran, Deepak Chopra. The masters don't see money or oil, they don't dwell in the material world like George W. Bush."

"I thought Bush was a spiritual man," I say.

"Bush is a dirt man. Born and raised looking at dirt, trying to find what's under that dirt and sell it to someone. Bush and Cheney. Dirt men. In Texas, people have oil and people have guns. Bad combination. They see a few John Wayne movies, and the whole world's in trouble."

The sock vendor laughs.

"Doesn't that make you angry?" I ask.

"It used to. Anger is a natural emotion and it always comes around, but you have to be higher than base emotions, rise above them or they will rule you. Just like the government."

"What is your name?" I ask.

"Why?"

"I'm writing something and I want to include you."

"Please don't do that."

"Why not?"

"A little knowledge is a dangerous thing, my brother. Teach someone a little bit of truth and he can become Father Divine, who set up shop right here on Broad Street, at the Divine Lorraine, and had people worship him as if he was God. You tell the wrong people some secrets of the universe, and if they have a large ego, a sick ego, only trouble will come of it."

"How do you know so much?" I ask.

"An inner voice."

"An inner voice?"

"I was sitting in a movie theater in Center City when I was twenty-four years old and a voice came to me and told me: consciousness comes from consciousness; consciousness begets consciousness; and consciousness is God. That's all I needed to hear. That's all anyone needs to know. The rest is up to you."

"That must have been some movie. What was it?"

"I don't remember," he says.

What kind of question was that?

"I am walking Broad Street," I tell the vendor.

"These socks will help your walk."

"Where should I go? What should I avoid?" I ask.

"My brother, you take yourself wherever you go, so it doesn't really matter. You'll be all right. I see no evil in your heart. You're a good man. Have no fear. These socks can help. They have been blessed."

"Blessed?"

"I asked God to bless these socks. And he did."

I believe him. Tears fill my eyes. We embrace. I take a deep breath. He smiles. I buy some socks. Six pair for five dollars. White Excell Cushion Athletic Tube Socks. All cotton. I walk on. I am light-headed as I bop between Rush Street and Somerset and see Jackie Robinson sliding past Yogi Berra's tag. Safe! The mural on the brick wall is three stories high and so effective you half expect Yogi to jump up and down and scream obscenities at the umpire. Wait a minute. Jackie Robinson? What is Jackie doing here? This ain't Brooklyn. This is Broad Street, not Flatbush Avenue. Philly had no Jackie. No Willie, no Monte, no Campy, no Newk. No African-Americans were invited onto the baseball diamonds of Philadelphia until it was too embarrassing to keep them off. (Of course, three Negro League World Series were played at the Baker Bowl, home of the Phillies for fifty-one years, just a few blocks south of this mural.)

The Phillies had no black players until 1957—a decade after Jackie broke the color barrier. You won't find his mural on any walls and you don't know his name. That was the whole idea. John E. Kennedy was a thirty-one-year-old journeyman when he pinch-hit for Solly Hemus in 1957 and then appeared in four more games, had zero hits and zero impact on the city, and that's how the Phillies liked it. They went through the motions of integration when it was god-awful apparent that they were the last segregated team in the National League. Just as the Whiz Kids of 1950 were the last all-white team to win a World Series. The 1950s saw the emergence of Willie Mays, Hank Aaron, Ernie Banks, Roy Campanella, Frank Robinson. The Phillies missed all of them, passed on several of them. They were white and they stunk. The Phillies had two winning seasons in the 1950s.

After the first game of the 1960 season, manager Eddie Sawyer called a press conference and said, "I'm forty-nine and I want to live to be fifty." He packed up and went home. Quit on the spot. He knew the future and it was bleak. The next season, the Phillies were an astounding 47 and 107.

Gene Mauch was the new manager. Comparisons to JFK were striking and immediate: young, charismatic, media-savvy, with great hair and dedication, a strategist. Nobody ever managed, or overmanaged, a game like Gene Mauch. It was thrilling to behold. Comparisons, conscious or not, to JFK were unavoidable. Smart, intense, vital, vigorous, cunning. Camelot's manager.

Then the Cuban Missile Crisis told us we were all going to die. And then the president did die. And then the 1960s began in earnest. And then Vietnam became a bloody quagmire. And then race riots torched North Philly in August of 1964. The ascendency of the Phillies, as much as anything else, spared the city a descent into utter bleakness. The miracle Phillies, there when you needed them, there to rescue your world, keep hope alive with Jim Bunning's perfect game in New York and Johnny Callison's three-run homer in the bottom of the ninth to win the All-Star game and Richie Allen, the Wampum Walloper, the wave of the future, the angry young man with an angrier bat, was on his way to both Rookie of the Year and MVP awards. Wow! What a time. What a season! The stars were aligned. Philadelphia was going to triumph. The city was never as alive and giddy and pouring a toast for destiny.

On September 20, 1964, the Phillies' record was 90-60. They had a 6½-game lead with twelve games to play. Nothing could stop them. No team in any sport had ever blown such a lead. You had to pinch yourself. And then pinch someone else just for the fun of it.

Ten days later, after ten straight losses, the Phillies were 90-70. And you were let in on the cruel joke. They were going to lose. The stars were aligned all right, aligned to rip out your guts and spit in your face. The Phils blew it. You blew it. We blew it. Lost in 1964 along with the pennant were such minor matters as faith, hope, charity, and the faint belief that anything would ever turn out right again. Hyperbole? Fuck you. You weren't there! Khrushchev, Lee Harvey Oswald, Chico Ruiz. (He stole home to beat the Phils 1–0. Stole home!) Assassination, race riots, the '64 Phillies. Such was life in the big city. A generation was deformed by the events of that fall. Two generations. All hope was specious. All glory was for others. You would never bank on a sure thing again.

It was only natural for Philadelphians to think the catastrophic collapse of '64 was some karmic payback for unnameable sins they had committed. When you are blessed, you feel fortunate. When you are cursed, you feel deserving. When the heavens offer salvation and then snatch it away at the last possible and most hideous moment, you figure you're guilty of something, something huge.

For Philadelphians over a certain age, "The '64 Phillies" remains a code for all things demoralizing, specious, underhanded, coercive, false, ruthless, misleading, cruel, insurmountable, unjust, rotten, and life altering, not in a positive way.

Looking up at Jackie Robinson sliding past Yogi Berra, I remember how my brother used to be convinced that that September was the beginning of his downward spiral. I call him.

"Do you still blame the '64 Phillies?"

"Now more than ever," he says.

"Why now more than ever?"

"I've had therapy to prove it."

"You were only what, thirteen?"

"It was like a bad bar mitzvah—today you are a loser, schmuck."

"Do you really remember that season?"

"Just the other day, I shared at a meeting how the first kilo I bought was called Chico Ruiz."

"Chico Ruiz?" I ask.

"It was so good it would steal your home and ruin your life."

"You don't blame the drugs? You blame the Phillies?"

"Gotta go, bro."

"Why?"

"The junkies need me."

On the northwest corner of Broad and Lehigh stands, somehow precariously, a colossus of a decayed factory that once housed Botany 500, a swanky men's clothing company. The ten-story monster speaks to big-city torpor, to manufacturing rot and global outsourcing, to the deterioration of industrial might that once buttressed North America and North Philly. As they did with many unused factories on Broad Street, squatters and junkies took over the lower floors of the Botany Building for an extended stay. A year ago, the 550,000-square-foot shell was scrubbed clean of humans and all manner of toxic materials, including asbestos. Zoned for industrial use, it can be yours for only $35 million. Temple University might want to lease some space for housing and the city has inquired about leasing office space, but the owner wants out, wants to the sell the whole pachyderm, not parts. If interested, contact Albert Nasser, who won the building when Botany 500 went belly-up and owed him a ton of money. Nasser is a Syrian who lives in Switzerland and makes his children's clothing, swimwear, and underwear in Hong Kong, the Philippines, India, Pakistan, Jordan, Egypt, Haiti, Guatemala, and Nicaragua and then sells to discount retailers unfriendly to unions. The international garmento has no use for a white elephant in the middle of a union town.

So there it sits, across the street from Brian Snyder. Brian Snyder opened Lehigh Pharmacy a decade ago and has been waiting, at first patiently, now impatiently, for someone other than junkies to occupy the huge hollow creature in whose shadow he toils. He knows the neighborhood, and his pharmacy, would benefit immediately, directly, but he doesn't know how long he can hold out. His pharmacy doesn't sell shampoo or sunglasses. It sells drugs. It's one small room with a few signs that say NO FOOD and it looks more like a prison dispensary than an apothecary. You have to slide your prescriptions under the double-thick glass windows and wait for a half hour on plastic chairs. With three Rite Aids in the general area, Snyder calls the competition "brutal," calls the health care system "brutal," and fears this writer will be "brutal" too. He wants to check my copy before I hand it in.

Ah, Philadelphians. Always finding the dark cloud surrounding the silver lining.

I outline the First Amendment to Brian, and explain how journalism generally functions. He is nervous. He wants to know what he can do to help the previous paragraph frame him in a positive manner. I mention a few tranquilizers he might find in his stockpiles and leave it at that.

Susquehanna Avenue is not an Indian term for "Never Elect a Mayor Named Street." It is an Algonquin word meaning "people of the muddy river." The Susquehannock were an indigenous people comprising five tribal groups. Bellicose, imperialistic, they were seven thousand strong when John Smith met them in 1608 and was impressed by their height and wide variety of weapons. By 1763, there were only twenty Susquehannock left, and they had all been converted by the Quakers and lived peacefully in Conestoga, Pennsylvania, outside Philly. Ongoing Indian wars outraged white settlers and, well, from a book called *First Nations* we find this account:

"As feelings rose, fourteen Susquehannock were arrested and placed in the jail for their own protection. A mob formed (known as the Paxton boys). They proceeded to the village at Conestoga, killed the six Susquehannock they found there, and burned the houses. Then they went to the jail, broke in, took the last fourteen Susquehannock the world would ever see . . . and beat them to death!"

Presently, I arrive at the stretch where, in my youth, the hookers would walk Broad. My mentor, Eliot Fisher, taught me how to pick up streetwalkers the summer I graduated high school. It's not all that difficult, but you'd like someone with experience to lay out the do's and don'ts. You worried about who was getting in your car or who might jump out of the shadows, but the dangers were more imagined than real; the extravagantly visible girls and their invisible pimps knew an untoward incident would cramp their style, and they were too smart to stem the flow of johns.

I had read *One Hundred Dollar Misunderstanding,* about a white boy and a black prostitute, primarily because it had been written by Robert Gover, a fellow alumnus of Girard College. While the novel had caused a scandal, breaking some serious taboos of the 1950s, it had also been championed by the likes of Norman Mailer and Gore Vidal, gaining both social significance and literary merit. All factors seem to bestow upon me a personal license; if to become a writer this was the price one had to pay, count me in.

Coming back from a Phillies game or following a successful night at Mosconi's pool hall, around ten or eleven, we'd cruise up and down this stretch of Broad Street and spy a tomato in a short skirt—Eliot called them tomatoes, hothouse, farm-ripened, or heirloom, anything but cherry, and never Jersey—and Eliot would signal her with a hissing "Pssst! Pssst!" Pushing wet air in short truncated streams through your closed front teeth made a sharp, vaguely sexual sound that could perforate any night. "Psssst! Psssst!" The tomatoes would walk over to the car to negotiate.

"How ya doin', babycakes?" she would ask.

"You got some time for us?" Eliot would ask back.

"You wanna go 'round the world?"

"How much for a blowjob?" he would ask.

"You a cop, baby?"

"Do I look like a cop, baby?"

"No, baby. I jest gotta ax."

Sometimes, one tomato took care of two johns. We would drive to a safe spot and take turns in the backseat. One night, I was in the front seat listening to the postgame show on the radio when Eliot tried to enter a tomato through her bottom.

"Whoa, babycakes, you cain't do that," I heard her say.

"I'll pay extra," said my mentor.

"It ain't a matter of money."

"Then what is it?"

"It's my back door. I be saving that for my husband."

Eliot tapped me on the shoulder and said, "You gotta love a girl with her priorities in order."

Properly indoctrinated, I cruised Broad Street solo. All you needed to reach manhood was a car and a twenty dollar bill.

6

No Child Left Behind

Dauphin Street to Cecil B. Moore Avenue

OLDIES BUT GOODIES
   by Grace Bauer

Because she's had more than her share
of sad stories and Molson's Ale,
she finds herself at midnight
circling the City of Brotherly Love
singing her heart out with the girl groups
playing on the radio.

The Chiffons do One Fine Day
like it's still 1963
and all the boys she dreamed
she'd fall in love with weren't dead
or gay or still strung out from Nam,
drinking off a rough divorce or looking
for a wife they think will look good
on their resumes.

To the fast-talking DJ
this is just a good night's work,
but he's doing a job on her.
Her head spins like a worn-out 45,
back to when she'd bump and grind
all night to The Temptations or The Miracles,
before she realized lost love
was worse than any lyric, when she still
wondered what the Kingsmen
really sang in Louie, Louie.

S M O K E Y Robinson and the Jackson Five used to perform on the stage of the Uptown Theater; now they are frozen murals, rendered by elementary school kids, near the darkened box office of this once great soul palace. Many people and much talk has tried to resurrect the Uptown, but all efforts have failed. The first show I ever saw here featured Major Lance, Mary Wells, and the Vibrations, and "introduced" the Supremes. Our seats were good enough that we could tell, my Temple fraternity brothers from AEPi and me, that Mary Wilson was sexier than skinny-minny Diana. We were the Jitterbugs, the White Negro Wannabes, sensing there was something truer and hipper, both culturally and spiritually, in the black world than our own; no flimflam, no existential drama: you be black, now deal with it. For boot camp training, we went to the local playgrounds and took mental notes, and physical lumps.

If pants are now big and baggy to demonstrate how the poor have to shoplift or hide weapons, back in the day we wore them too tight and too short to replicate hand-me-downs. The legs of our sweatpants and sleeves of our sweatshirts were jaggedly torn to affect faux poverty. Our suit jackets had no collars because the Tempts' had none. We let our hair grow 'fro, or, if we needed help, like Mike Schmidt, had it permed. And we wore Mays's 24—never Mantle's 7. Russell Simmons is not the first to take ghetto fashion to the white masses. Only the first to cash in.

Presently, on the corner near the Uptown, a kid of confirmation age waits for a bus. Could be any kid in any ghetto. His mother stands next to him. Could be any mother. They stand in silence, postures in antipathy to each other. The kid wears a gray work jacket that says STATE PROPERTY 18153, as if already in jail, or representin' someone already in jail—a family member? a best friend? a hip-hop hero?—or just preparing his mother for the day he goes away. You like how I look, Mama? Get used to it. Ten percent of all African-American males end up incarcerated. There are more black men in prison than college. We are nurturing more kids in downtown America resigned to crime, designing to do us harm, than terrorists from without. This is the only fashion statement that matters, Mama!

Prison uniforms, created by Jay-Z's Rocawear, are both parody and protest, approach and avoidance, the way military gear was for anti-war hippies and veterans alike. Beanie Sigel, the rap star, is the titular designer of the State Property line. This is part of his sales pitch: "You know how you put your gun in your waistline and you gotta worry about it slipping? With these clothes, you don't got to worry about that. Don't worry about having to run from the police neither, because State Property can stand the search."

Apparently not. Beanie Sigel's third album was released before he was—Sigel was serving time on federal gun and drug charges, and facing a retrial on attempted murder, allegedly repeatedly shooting a dude outside the Pony Tail Bar, a Philly strip club. (He was acquitted.)

Beanie Sigel was born Dwight Grant thirty-two years ago on Sigel Street in South Philly. His biggest hit tune was "Hard Knock Life," sampling a song from Broadway's *Annie*. He starred in the feature films *State Property* and *State Property 2*. (Unindictable crimes.)

"Come on, James," says the mother of the little prison boy when the bus arrives. "Let's not miss this bus."

"Yes, Mama," says James, and they board the C bus heading south. From the chimney of the bus, #5488, black soot billows.

Who can resist a pretzel, one of those soft oversized pretzels eaten with mustard—not cinnamon, not sugar, not raisins, not jalapeño, not almonds, not nothing from Auntie Anne's or Granny Smith's or your frozen food department. Salt and mustard. That's it. And you never let the vendor slather the mustard on your pretzel. To get the perfect coating, *you* squeeze the mustard onto the pretzel following its figure-eight, then raise the pretzel to shoulder height, snap your wrist as if choosing out, odds versus evens, or throwing a curveball, and just the right amount of mustard will adhere to the salty pretzel as the excess decorates the sidewalk or street. Philadelphians don't mind a little spicy mustard on the street, close to the curb, please.

Such a well-dressed madeleine reminds me of hanging out at the corner candy store with my brother, so I call him.

"I can't talk," he says.

"What's the matter?" I ask.

"Just got out of therapy."

"Bad session?"

"No. Bad childhood."

"What was the session about?" I ask.

"Her."

"Her who?"

"You know who. The paramour."

"Tell me about it."

"I wish I could, but I can't."

"Why not?"

"It involves her."

"So?"

"She won't let me."

"Won't let you what?"

"Talk to you about her."

"Just talk about yourself."

"She's very involved in this little drama," he says.

"Disguise her identity."

"She considers all this very private."

"All what?"

"What I can't talk to you about."

"Pretend I'm a priest. Brother Bruce."

"I can't talk to anyone about it—not a priest, not the shrink, and definitely not you."

"What would happen if you told me?"

"Then you would know."

"Know what?"

"What I'm not allowed to say and you're not allowed to know."

"What's that?"

"How she treats me."

"How does she treat you?"

"Like this."

"Like what?"

"Like I can't talk to my own brother about how she treats me."

"Why did you promise?"

"Did I have a choice?"

"Yes. Of course. You always have a choice."

"When she told me I couldn't talk to any blondes . . ."

"You had a choice."

"When she said I couldn't sleep with her on work nights . . ."

"You had a choice."

"When she said I had to see her therapist or we were finished . . ."

"You had a choice."

"Then why do I see her therapist?"

"You live in California."

"If I betray her, we're finished."

"If talking to your brother is a betrayal, you're already finished."

"She was betrayed by someone close to her when she was young."

"I feel sorry for her. That was a long time ago."

"She's convinced me to keep all matters between us a secret."

"But you're telling me about the rules she has made for you."

"Am I in trouble?"

"Zugswang."

"Gesundheit."

"Remember zugswang?" I ask.

"From our Hitler Youth days?"

"No, playing chess. It's when any move you make puts you into a worse position than you're already in."

"Danke. I'm in zugswang and I can't even tell anyone."

"You can tell me," I tell him.

"I can't. She says what goes on between us stays between us."

"You know who she sounds like?"

"An ad for Las Vegas."

"No."

"Who?"

"You really don't know?" I ask.

"No! Who?"

"Her."

"Her who?"

"Her!"

"Really?"

"Really."

"Mom?"

"Mom."

"Shit. Why did you call?"

"Something about a soft pretzel."

"You said a mouthful."

"So I guess you're not getting married next month?" I ask.

"The horah. The horah."

Our mother was so secretive she would disapprove of me writing that she was secretive, even now, five years after her permanent exit from the scene. I can still see her, feel her, deliver her patented death glare across the room, across decades of therapy, across the universe in order to silence me. She relied on the death glare whenever I was too far away to be kicked. Sometimes, she executed a fierce one-two glare-kick combo, most often resulting in a TKO.

One Thanksgiving, for example, my aunt asked why my brother was not at the turkey dinner and I began to tell her that he was in Israel, on a kibbutz, which I thought would fill her and everyone else at the holiday table with pride. Suddenly, I received the ol' one-two, the Look and the Kick.

"He's living on a ki—ouch!—a, eh, canoe, in a river, somewhere on some water. Please pass the sweet potatoes with marshmallows," I said. The family knew my mother's propensity toward secretiveness and respected it; she was a single mother long before that term existed, and while it elicited empathy, understanding was another matter. No one pushed any buttons. Everyone had something to be ashamed of, something they did not want on the table, even at, or especially at, a family dinner. The turkey was stuffed with shame. Evasion was perverted into kindness.

After dinner, I asked my mother why she gave me the old one-two.

"It's nobody's business," she said.

"She's your sister. It's our family."

"Then she'll want to know how he got the money to go to Israel."

"So?"

"I don't want her to know he sells drugs."

"She knows, Mom. Everyone knows."

If anyone had any doubts that my brother had been dealing pot since high school, and doing it very well, all doubts were erased the

night the front door came crashing down and the police arrested my
mother and brother as she was doing the dishes and he was cleaning
the twigs and stems from an ounce. Four officers entered the house
with drawn guns. When two started running up the stairs to the second floor, my mother protested.

"You can't go up there," she snarled, expecting them to defer to her
admonishment as everyone else did. They searched the second floor.
They found nothing there and missed the pound of weed in the vac-
uum cleaner bag in the downstairs closet. The ounce on the table was
enough for the bust.

"Can I get dressed?" asked my mother.

"What are you wearing underneath that?" asked one cop, referring
to her housedress.

"Look," she said as she opened her housedress, displaying her bra
and underpants.

After a night in jail, with hooks and crooks, as she referred to her
fellow inmates, the judge apologized for imprisoning a fifty-five-year-
old woman who was employed, owned her own house, and had never
been in trouble before. Though ever feisty on the surface, my
mother's world had been cracked apart, and she sold her home and
moved to an apartment in Center City shortly after the bust. It began
the sanest, if loneliest, period of her life.

How do I know that? My mother kept a secret diary, unseen by
anyone until after her death. Thirty books with daily entries from
1970 through 1999. At first, I couldn't stop reading them. I went to
the dates I remembered: birthdays, holidays, important days. I know
she wanted them to be read because there were additions and correc-
tions added years later, with new dates. Her own private Talmud, ex-
panded and reconsidered with new opinions and insights. She seldom
wrote on politics or world events. Often, she was sad about AIDS or
people in prison for drugs or victims of natural disasters.

But in her 1975 diary, she loved Jackie Kennedy for being so beautiful and graceful. She hated Jackie Kennedy for being stoic, so tear-

less during her husband's funeral, an unmatchable exemplar for widows of the world. Little did my mother know that Jackie had contemplated suicide, had been unable to function, was fortunate to have family enough and money enough to see her through, not to mention unlimited medications. How well my mother knew her similarities to Jackie: both lost their husbands suddenly with two young kids, and were forced to find professions, and men; dalliances and affairs were ended by a short, unattractive rich man from far away. For Jackie, Onassis the Greek shipping tycoon. For my mother, Klapner the Brooklyn camera salesman. Only Klapner was married and never got unmarried and didn't die and leave her millions. He helped out with the rent and took her on business trips to Florida and New Orleans.

After reading in her diaries about her orgasms and Klapner's orgasms, I decided to stop reading the diaries and mail one book, chosen at random, to thirty different relatives.

Dear Aunt Ethel,
 Here's 1978. Rough year for Mom. Hope you enjoy it.
  Love, Bruce.

Dear Uncle Mike,
 Here's 1993. You are not mentioned. Not once. Guess Mom didn't think of you that year.
  Love, Bruce.

I thought better of shipping my mother, piecemeal, around the country in order to lighten my own burden. So I kept the diaries, half read, half unread, in an old suitcase in the room of the grandson she loved less than her other grandson.

Within a year, a diary by my Uncle Joe's brother, Israel Chanin, was discovered and exhibited at the Philadelphia Jewish Archives Center. It was an exciting discovery for the center, a 430-page diary of a Russian immigrant teenage boy written in his native Yiddish. Rare are diaries of males, rarer still by an intelligent, eloquent male who details his family's odyssey from Lithuania through China and San Francisco to Philadelphia. He wrote about the topics of the day, Lenin's death in 1925 and the sentencing of Sacco and Vanzetti in 1927, but primarily stuck to Philadelphia life, family dynamics, left-wing politics, and a particular five-day hunger strike for the mistreated workers. I remember Izzy as a family doctor in the worst Newark, New Jersey, ghetto.

When visiting the Jewish Archives one day, I joked about my mother's quotidian diary going on exhibition. They didn't laugh. They were wild for every one of the thirty volumes. All the elements I thought mediated against its novelty or value were its very attractions: because she was an ordinary woman, an older Jewish woman living alone in a major metropolis at the tail end of the twentieth century, writing about family and shopping and medical misadventures, she was an anthropologist's dream girl. The hoi polloi are not often represented in hotsy totsy places, as my mother might have said.

The ironies were too rich to pass up—soon, my secretive mother's secretive life will be on display for everyone to see.

I have walked three miles or four. My quads ache. My dogs bark. I think of the thousands of normal folk who finish the Broad Street Run every May Day, from Somerville Avenue to the Navy Yard, all ten miles. The record is less than an hour—45 minutes, 16 seconds. For ten miles! I muzzle my dogs. Shhhhhh. Down boys, down. Yo, there's Grover Washington Jr.! God rest his soul, of which he had plenty. I've always looked up to Grover, but not from this angle. He must be sixty feet high, in a colorful dashiki. His eyes are shut and he's blowing a glittering twenty-foot saxophone in his own dreamworld. His nimbus must be fifteen feet wide. Looks like a burnt umber halo. Funny, if anyone knew how hard it was to be a saint in the city, it was Grover. I co-produced a concert (and video) at the Academy of Music with Grover and an all-star group. He was a great player and a joy to work with. Donny Osmond directed the taping. You should have seen the two of them, Mr. Magic and the Mormon, vamping on "Just the Two of Us." Grover knew it was hard to be a latter-day saint in the city too.

Muralist Peter Pagast says he painted a spotlight, not a halo. He also says he didn't know Grover from a hole in the wall, never heard him play a note, and has no opinion about the man or his music. He is one of the few, for Grover irritated purists as he inspired devotees. Hailed and criticized for founding "smooth jazz," Grover was a master of R&B jazz or jazz funk or blues pop or funky blues fusion. For his splendid version of Bob Marley's "Jammin'," throw in reggae and gospel too. And he collaborated with singers Bill Withers and Phyllis Hyman. Hell, Coltrane played with vocalist Johnny Hartman. Say what you might, Grover could blow, and his *Winelight* CD remains a classic and should not be blamed for the skanky imitators it spawned, led by the soprano-sucking Kenny G.

Painting the Grover mural was an assignment for Peter Pagast, as were Edgar Allan Poe and Paul Robeson and José Carreras and Thomas Eakins. Have brush (and ladder), will travel. Pagast spends a month at the wall, on scaffolding, painting with Nova Color, a special unguent with extra pigment and weather resistance. Pagast works for the Murals Art Program (MAP) and here's how it works: using photographs and money provided by Grover's widow, Pagast did a 16 x 20 inch thumbnail that was approved by Grover's family, the Diamond Street Association, and the Murals Art Program director. The director is Jane Golden, and she has overseen 2,700 murals and has 1,000 more walls in waiting. So successful has the program been that community leaders from all over the country hold conventions to find out how Jane Golden pulled this off, how she painted parking lots and put up some paradise. Ooh-la-la-la-la-la.

In 1984, Golden was hired by the city to reach out to graffiti artists and redirect their talents, harness their energies. A decade later, Murals Art Program was a force—the largest employer of artists, a respected agency in revitalizing hoods (human and neighbor), adding about one hundred new murals a year, giving Philadelphia the most outdoor art in the world. The murals are assigned from on high, but are sanctioned by each community before paint hits wall. Mural subjects run the gamut from Quaker founders to Larry Fine, one of the Three Stooges. Chinese idols, Mexican workers, a cop who died in Iraq, historical figures, fantasies, a three-hundred-foot healing wall along railroad tracks, triptychs, groups real and groups imagined, rural murals and urban dreams.

When San Francisco wants to honor someone, they create the Church of John Coltrane. In Philly, murals suffice. You won't find the Beth El Jack Klugman or the Church of Dr. J.

Arriving at the Temple University Main Campus, you wonder "Where is the Temple University Main Campus?" Where's the quad? The gardens? The homecoming queens? Where are the students engaged in Socratic discussions or naked parties? A few stray students disappear into a subway kiosk as a half dozen others shuffle across Broad Street carrying books, some with scarlet T decals. You can't believe that 32,877 students are learning from 2,361 teachers behind these facades, this architectural hodgepodge with nothing holding it together except Broad Street. Structures stand side by side like brothers from another mother: a sleek, modern building rubs shoulders with a medieval abbey. Food trucks are lined up in front of a gaggle of row houses.

So sheltered was my youth that only when I saw the campuses of Berkeley and Duke (while scouting for my sons) did I realize how ugly Temple University had been—is—and how impoverished were my college days, in aesthetics and academics. In my first semester, I learned high-stakes pinochle from my AEPi brothers and memorized every detail, from the inside out, of Judy Dentine's baby blue Corvette convertible. From my second go-round, a few years later, after a few LSD trips that seemed to last longer than my first marriage, I can remember

Donna Debs's lips in the darkened fire escape, Joan Horvath's lips on the bright roof of the *Temple News*, and Chuck Newman's journalism class. He gave me no lip at all, only encouragement.

That's the accumulated knowledge retained from four years at university.

Temple is like a great lovable state-sponsored hooker: cheap, easy to enter, amenable to any course of study, and always available on Broad Street. All you have to do is give up on football and meals from any place without wheels.

Karen Carpenter drives to school every day and eats lunch at one of the omnipresent grease trucks. Like 77 percent of her fellow Owls, she is a home-stater. Unlike anyone else, she is a third-year film student who graduated Tyler Art back in 1987, played bass in a punk group called Plumbing, and then realized she could pour all her various passions into filmmaking.

"It is a great medium because you can tell a story with visuals and music and writing. You get to use all of it. And you're not in a room all alone being depressed and wondering if what you're doing is any good."

Awards say her latest short film is doing well, winning the Hamptons Film Festival and accepted in Torino, Italy. Carpenter will be sending her short to seventy festivals all told. It is about a young girl from a small town (Carpenter hails from New Bloomfield, Pennsylvania) who smokes (Carpenter did), drinks (still does), and curses (fuck yeh) and has to leave her hometown in order to maintain, or find, her sanity.

The film is called *My Scarlet Letter.*

The final line written across the screen is: "My Scarlet Letter is the invisible badge that reminds me that wherever I go, I came from here."

I gaze upon the hundred-foot banner waving across Broad Street with the scarlet T hyping Temple football; it is the only gonfalon the football program will be flying for a long time. It should be at half-mast. "Tickets are still available at 215-204-5040." They will cost $240 for the best seats, and spiral down to $50 and $25. There will be plenty of seats available at Lincoln Field. Why? Because Temple stinks, stinks so bad it was voted the worst team in the nation by an ESPN poll, "The Bottom Ten."

Temple football has had no winning seasons since 1990 and only two since 1980, and they were modest. Jerry Berendt took over with high hopes and a master plan in 1989. Went 1-10. After going 11-33, he was gone. Ron Dickerson took over in 1993 with high hopes and a master plan. He went 1-10 in his first year. After going 8-47, he was gone. Bobby Wallace took over in 1998 with high hopes and a master plan. He was gone after eight seasons and a 19-66 record. Al Golden took his place. Lord have mercy. This season, under Golden, the Owls lost to Louisville and Minnesota on consecutive weeks by identical scores: 62–0. They allowed a point every minute of the game. They gave up 124 points while accumulating none. Zero. The opponents had all the X's and Temple had all the O's. And there are no signs of improvement. Temple was thrown out of the Big East last year and maybe Division 1-A this year and perhaps the continent known as North America next year.

Things have not turned out the way they were drawn up on the blackboard.

That I am only an almost-alum (needing a few science courses to graduate) does not stop me from looking for Temple scores on a dozen Saturdays every winter and feeling a chill wind; "we" were in a rebuilding mode when I attended Temple. When you are putrid in public for such a long time, it adversely affects the image of the school, the enrollment, the faculty, the city, even the taste of cheesesteaks. Why can't an institution of higher learning solve a problem that has been conquered by LSU and Florida State and schools in cold cities and big cities and big, cold Eastern cities, and damn, what is the problem with Temple U? Wouldn't it be better for the school to simply scrap the nightmare of big-time football and concentrate on something positive?

If a student had passing grades in only two classes for thirty years, wouldn't a compassionate counselor recommend an alternative career path? Maybe in a kitchen somewhere, or a food truck?

Take Temple football. Please. Please!

If Allen Ginsberg were matriculating here, and aware of football, he might be enraged enough, disgusted enough, to ululate a poem thusly:

OWL

I saw the best bodies of my generation destroyed by
the Big East, pride stripped naked,
dragging themselves off the field at dusk
looking for an angry goalpost,
helmeted hip-hopsters churning for the ancient heavenly
connection to the defensive dynamo in the X's and O's,
who pass-rushed blitz-eyed and high stared up
into the stands of Lincoln superboxes,
saw darkness of backfield flats floating across the tips
of fingers concentrating on interception,
who bared their brawn to Heaven above the subway and
saw JoPa's angels staggering over goal lines illuminated,
who passed through universities with radiant winning records
hallucinating Louisville and Navy and long bomb strategies
among the euphemism of cherry and white war,
who were expelled from the academic conference for lazy &
lopsided obscene scores on the Saturday afternoon skull,
who cowered in unlockered rooms in underwear,
burning their scholarships in wastebaskets and listening
to the razzmatazz through the wall . . .
Blocking dummies! Mad generation! down on
the last quarter of Time!
Real holy laughter in the huddle! They saw it all!
the gang tackles! the holy fumbles! They bade farewell!

They jumped offsides! to solitude! waving!
yelling at zebras! carrying flowers! into the street!
That broad Broad Street!

What used to be called Columbia Avenue is now Cecil B. Moore. The civil rights leader championed a wide range of causes, including the integration of schools, trade unions, and city jobs. He served on the City Council and was president of the local NAACP chapter when all hell was breaking loose, from 1963 to 1967, and is officially credited with helping to restore order after the Columbia Avenue Riots in the summer of '64. During his tenure, NAACP membership grew from seven thousand to fifty thousand within a few years. Cecil B. Moore is perhaps best remembered by the city, and me, as leading the pickets and protesters at the wall of Girard College in order to desegregate that institution, my alma mater. I remember Cecil. Up close and personal. With a soapbox preacher's delivery and a lawyer's command of the language, Cecil would lead the twenty or thirty "freedom fighters" at the front gate of Girard College as the boys went to school and were in school and I remember spring days, sitting in English class on the third floor of the high school listening to lessons about Shakespeare and looking out and over the wall to see Cecil and his army marching with placards and listening to their chants of equality—and I wasn't the only one looking, as the local folks sitting on their front stoops would watch the show and I couldn't help but take particular notice of young black boys sitting next to their fathers; their neighborhood was squalid, their own houses falling apart, their fathers were out of work and barely literate, in my imagination, and as I sat there half absorbing the iambic pentameter machinations of Lady Macbeth, I felt only one thing: I was envious of those boys. What I would trade for the comfort of sitting on a crumbling stoop next to my father.

The boys beyond the wall wanted what I had. I wanted what they had. Life is always better on the other side of the wall, the wall of history, the wall of fear, the wall of illusion.

The faculty and the students were foursquare against integration, for all the obvious and invisible reasons; change is embraced by few. I felt isolated in my hope that Cecil B. Moore would, after years and years of struggle, break the chains and start sending black boys to my school. It was only right. Anyone could see that. I could see that. We were cozily protecting this verdant oasis in the midst of an urban sandstorm. All the talk about wills was hypocrisy: insiders knew Stephen Girard's book-length will had been broken dozens of times and Girard's intention, as he stated, was to provide for the poor and needy of his community by leaving large sums of money to a large number of charities, and many millions for the establishment of America's first residential school for disadvantaged children, for "poor white male orphans, of legitimate birth and good character between the ages of six and ten."

When Girard died in 1831, there were seven thousand African-Americans in Philadelphia. Some free, some enslaved. Considering his times, gainsaying nothing, one can neither charge Girard with racism nor assume he would do the same today.

When the Pennsylvania Supreme Court defended the school policy in 1956, decreeing that any man had the liberty to his bias, and the sacrosanctity of his will, the case went to the U.S. Supreme Court. Eventually, after a decade of litigation, after Martin Luther King visited the wall, after the hands of time struggled forward, African-Americans were permitted entrance. And then girls. And the "fatherless" was changed to "one-parent." And the alumni fought tooth and nail every step of the way. I have not been back to Girard since I graduated.

It was not the first case involving Girard College to reach the highest court. Girard's family attempted to prevent the construction of the school before it was ever built. A thick tome, Girard's last will and testament detailed every stipend to his slaves, every dollar to charities, every brick of every building and each course to be taught in his beloved school, going so far as, though he was no architect or pedagogue, to dictate the thickness and height of the stone wall that would surround the forty-four-acre institution, the type of marble for various roofs, the exact dimensions of rooms, the number of instructors, and the single class of persons banned from ever stepping foot on his campus: clergymen.

Of the thousands upon thousands of words he wrote by hand, a single paragraph caused so much public scandal and familial consternation that the will was contested by his heirs and landed before the Supreme Court of the United States.

"I enjoin and require that no ecclesiastic, missionary or minister of any sect whatsoever, shall ever hold or exercise any duty whatsoever in the said college; nor shall any such person ever be admitted for any purpose, or as a visitor, within the premises appropriated to the purposes of the said college. . . . I desire to keep the tender minds of orphans free from the excitements which clashing doctrines and sectarian controversy are so apt to produce."

Public outrage! What an infidel, this foreigner! His heirs in France hired the redoubtable Daniel Webster, orator, U.S. senator, secretary of state, to halt this travesty—and keep the millions of dollars, estimated at $30 billion in today's currency, for their own purposes. Webster delivered a stirring defense of Christianity in his summation by arguing that the proposed college should not be built at all, due to its prohibition not only of teaching the Bible but from the exclusion of men of the cloth.

"No good can be looked for from this college," declaimed Webster. "If Girard had desired to bring trouble, and quarrel, and struggle upon the city, he could have done it in no more effectual way. The plan is unblessed in design and unwise in purpose. If the court should set it aside, and I be instrumental in contributing to that result, it will be the crowning mercy of my professional life."

In a unanimous decision, the Court ruled against Webster and the Girards, saying that just because the school did not promote Deism was no reason to deny its existence; moreover, no truly Christian country should prohibit any school that prohibits Christian teaching.

Eighteen forty-four. The Age of Enlightenment!

The nonsectarian gates of the school—gates designed by Stephen Girard—were opened to the first students in January 1848. The study course—designed by Stephen Girard—included reading, writing, arithmetic, astronomy, philosophy, French, and Spanish.

I walked through those gates in January 1954, a century and six years later.

7

THE KID HAS NO LEFT
(A CINEMATIC INTERLUDE)

Blue Horizon™

B ET WEEN Thompson and Master, at 1314 Broad Street, across from the massive prisonlike William Penn High School, is the Blue Horizon boxing club. It's a catering hall, community center, and a few other things too, but boxing is its calling card and the reason I'll be back this weekend.

EXT. BLUE HORIZON—FRIDAY NIGHT
The journalist gets in a long line that slowly slithers down Broad and deposits him at the front doors. Close-up of the sign on each door:

NO WEAPONS ALLOWED
(LAW ENFORCEMENT INCLUDED)
NO FOOD OR DRINKS OR CAMERAS

(Law enforcement is included parenthetically because club boxing attracts men who spend their spare time in gyms and use their muscles professionally; men with prominent jaws and tattoos and broken noses and T-shirts advertising their affiliations: police, security, servicemen.)

INT. BLUE HORIZON—NIGHT

If there was not a boxing ring in the middle of the auditorium, you would expect to see a Quaker elementary school talent show. The balconies are steep and the wood is hand-carved and there is a stage at the distant end of the hall. Each of the eight antique chandeliers sports burned-out bulbs, but no one can reach them or cares to. Directly above the ring are new ultra-bright lights. There is a good chance the old fixtures have been hanging here since the Loyal Order of Moose erected the auditorium in 1914.

The words Blue Horizon, with the little ™ in tow, are everywhere—along the balustrades, on signs, on ring posts, on the mat—as if anyone could forget, or is here for any other reason. The galleries are filled with gesticulating spectators, calling to mind the unsentimental Eakins paintings in which all the unlit doctors are watching a brightly illuminated surgery; it is an infelicitous image, born perhaps from the fact that Eakins was a Philadelphian, through and through.

Blood is inevitable, so everyone close to the fighters—referees, cutmen, cornermen—wears the powder blue elastic latex gloves you don't like to see your doctor slap on. The effect is modern minstrel show. The gloves are mandated by state law, along with the following equipment supplied by the promoter:

—Boxing gloves in GOOD condition.

—A gong or bell of size and resonance so as to be clearly heard.

—A complete set of numbered round cards.

—An ambulance and emergency personnel with emergency equipment that are available at all times during the event.

—A portable resuscitator with oxygen and appropriate endotracheal tubes and qualified operator.

—Adequate security.

INT. SECOND BOUT—NIGHT
Elad "Kosher Pit Bull" Shmouel easily outboxes Rasheed Daniels in a
four-round welterweight tilt. No one schleps all the way from Tel
Aviv to lose to a schmuck with a 3-10 record. The crowd of five hundred is very pleased and vocal about it. Testosterone fills the air as
cigar smoke would have ten years ago, or fifty. Squint and you're in
an old black and white movie with Kirk Douglas and Arthur
Kennedy. The crowd is 70 percent white and 80 percent male.
There are quite a few couples here on dates.

INT. FLASHBACK—DUSK
Split screen: Jewish male in his thirties is talking on the phone to a
pretty shiksa still at work in an office.

MAN
What are you doing Friday night?

WOMAN
Not much, why?

MAN
Wanna go see half-naked men pummel each other?

WOMAN
And then grab a bite to eat?

MAN
Sure, babe. Seven bouts and we're out.

WOMAN
Anyone I ever heard of?

MAN
Not likely.

WOMAN
Should I wear something special?

MAN
You know what I like.

WOMAN
You got that right.

MAN
You're a knockout, babe.

INT. BLUE HORIZON—NIGHT
People are dressed neither up nor down; it's Ocasional Nuevo, attire for a bistro or an AA meeting. If the men are not shy about showing off their physiques, the women are equally uninhibited. You glance. This is not the place where you stare at another man's woman. Or women. You glance again. The dude in the next row has two bountiful babes with him, one on each arm; the muscle shirt he wears does not cover much of his well-defined torso; to say he has tattoos on his shoulders and biceps would be like saying Seurat put little dots on a canvas. These landscapes are 360 degrees of bold colors and fine details, as if the French Impressionist had an overpowering urge to paint the Loire Valley when he couldn't get to an easel, so he settled for skin.

EXT. FANTASY SEQUENCE—DAY
Georges Seurat sticks colorful needles into a muscular fellow while two women romp smuttily in the countryside with a nameless journalist in a yellow straw hat.

INT. BLUE HORIZON—CONT.

Close-ups of mouths booing. More close-ups of more mouths boo-ing, with an occasional oratory outburst from the balcony highlight-ing the deficiencies of a particular boxer. The appositely named Mike McFail inspires such declamation. He is now fighting William Boggs, a local kid who has yet to lose.

McFail looks demented or drunk, staggering before he ever gets hit, and then swings ferociously, striking more air than opponent. You fear for his safety. He is thirty-three. McFail has won only twelve of his forty-one professional fights. He will not win tonight. You think he should be given some potent antidepressants and shown a new career path.

But every time McFail is about to go down, after absorbing multi-ple jabs that jelly his legs, he finds emergency energy and swings crazily and lands a punch and the score gets closer and the crowd livelier. The Romans want blood. They boo McFail for amateurish-ness, then boo Boggs for not knocking McFail's block off, then switch allegiance again, hailing McFail's tenacity, then delighting in Boggs's hot-dogginess. The joint is jumping and this is only the third bout and of no import.

Ring Magazine voted the Blue Horizon the best place in the country to watch boxing, and you know why: every seat is so good that you can smell the sweat, see the blood spurting as if from a garden soaker hose. You are in a barn watching a cockfight with bizarro reverse propor-tions: the combatants are human-size and the onlookers cocks.

Watching fights is exhausting: you keep anticipating, fearing, hoping, dreading that someone will make a mistake, a misstep, a bob instead of a weave, and the split-second error will cost him, cost him dearly, God forbid permanently. The tension drains the spectators.

Boggs beats McFail in a close decision. The boos beat the cheers in another close decision.

The judges earn $75 for each bout, and $10 more if the contest is televised. Refs get paid $100. The on-site doctor $150. The fees are set by the State Boxing Commission. "Drug tests are performed on a random basis—cost to the promoter is $21 per boxer, paid by check after the event."

Everyone knows who is supposed to win each fight before the opening bell. The winner will be the local kid, the kid with the better record, the up-and-comer using the older nowhere man as boxing fodder.

INT. DRESSING ROOM—NIGHT

The three card girls add more makeup and higher heels and change from ultra-short denim skirts to revealing Filene's dresses. The girls are each round's foreplay. The skimpier their outfits, the more serious the bout. And the more rowdy the crowd. The brief walk around the 20 x 20 foot ring gives the girls precious little time to strut their stuff. When they wave to the crowd, many men take it personally. So do the card girls.

INT. RING—NIGHT

Max Alexander takes on Tiwon Taylore in a light heavyweight bout. Alexander is young, strong, smart, undefeated, and local. Tiwon Taylore must be thirty-five with a 24-12-1 record and resides in Las Vegas. Guess who wins? Right. Guess who makes more money? Wrong. Taylore will have a bigger payday, precisely because it is a payday for him, not the stepping-stone it is for Alexander. Guess who made this match? Max Alexander's manager, Robert Bryant. That's how the game works. The Blue Horizon gave the "home" boxer the right to make the match, and a certain number of tickets to sell or distribute. With those moneys, the manager will pay his own boxer and the guest boxer too. Tiwon Taylore will get around $2,500 for his effort. The winner, the manager's boy, will get less.

INT. BLUE HORIZON—CONT.

On the way back from the lavatory, after the fifth bout, the writer passes the refreshment stand, where customers are lined up three deep. The prices are as simple as the menu: PRETZEL $1, HOT DOG $2, SAUSAGE $3, BEER $4.

Back in his seat, the writer can't shake the smell of the mustard and urine as he watches boxers trying to pound each other into veal marsala.

INT. RING—NIGHT
Gentleman Chazz Witherspoon, cousin of Philly-born Terrible Tim Witherspoon, almost immediately pounds his opponent into submission. It is a methodical, dispassionate pounding. The sounds are operatic. Fortissimo, staccato, martellato. The poor victim loses his mouthpiece three times, and his gloves have to be relaced and the stalling costs him a point and saves him thousands of brain cells. He will be hit by fifty or sixty shots to the head and body. If he fights eight times this year, and fought eight times last year and ten next year, the math does not add up in his favor. Nothing adds up. The writer is surprised he is not repulsed by the close-up brutality, that he actually gets caught up in the athleticism and the competition enough to stop obsessing about Muhammad Ali's slowly disintegrating body, or Joe Frazier's quickly disintegrating finances, or the grotesqueness of the fight game. If time and civilization have eclipsed this ancient test of men, what are all these people still doing here? Who watches all the fights on HBO and Showtime and ESPN and pay-per-view?

The main event pits Terrance "Heat" Cauthen against Joshua "Poison" Onyango. Heat is from Trenton, Poison from Uganda. The writer doesn't know the outcome of this one. And he doesn't care.

EXT. BLUE HORIZON—NIGHT
The writer exits. Takes a deep breath. Fights depression. Heads for the nearest bar.

8

No Orphan Left Untouched

Thompson Street to Girard Avenue

O N the northwest corner of Broad and Thompson is a plain
stand-alone one-story building that houses the Interstate
Blood Bank. A makeshift sign advertises: ALL DONORS $20
NOW. It's 3:30 P.M. The two dozen black plastic chairs are empty. It's
too nice a day for people to sell their precious blood. There is no one
behind the double-thick impenetrable windows, so I knock. Loudly.
A nurse in a white uniform appears and signals the bank is closed for
the day. I pantomime that I have a question. The nurse opens one of
the windows.

"We are closed for the day," she says.

"No volunteers?" I ask.

"We close when we reach our limit."

"How many is that?"

"Today? Ninety-something. It's always between eighty and a hundred pints of blood."

"You get eighty to one hundred people selling their blood every
day?" I repeat.

"Five days a week, fifty-two weeks a year. We turn lots of people away. Like you. I'm sorry."

"Oh, I'm not here for that," I say.

"If you're over eighteen and weigh more than a hundred pounds, you qualify. Tomorrow."

"No testing?" I ask.

"We test the blood for syphilis, AIDS, hepatitis B, hep C, and other communicable diseases. I have to go now."

"Where?" I ask.

"To test the blood, and label it, store it, deliver it. Come back to-morrow."

"Do I need anything when I come back?"

"A photo ID and Social Security card. If you come back tomorrow, you can't donate again for two months."

"Thank you," I say.

"See you tomorrow," she says. "Seven-thirty sharp."

I must look worse than I think.

If they prick ninety folks a day, on average, five days a week, and do not accept repeat donors for fifty-eight days, then approximately 3,608 different persons sell their blood for $20 a pop during a two-month span at this one site. There are nine other sites. Seems like a lot of blood peddling in Philadelphia in the dawn of the twenty-first century.

The street sign says Girard Avenue. I take a deep breath. Girard used to be synonymous with power and wealth in this town. Girard Bank. Girard Estates. Girard Trust. Girard Park. Girard Row. Girard College. It has all but been elided from public consciousness. Not mine. Seeing the very word feels like magic mushrooms have just kicked in. The McDonald's, the KFC, and the Checkers (two burgers for $3!) become blurry and then evaporate. I hear people passing by yet I cannot see them as I sink into the quicksand of involuntary memory. Girard. I want to run away. I stand as still as marble. I want to run now as I wanted to then, when I was young, when I was nine and twelve and fifteen, when I stood on this corner, after Thanksgiving or Christmas holiday, after a summer recess or a Sunday on the town, and now, as then, I am prevented from running by the unanswerable question: to where?

There is only here—whether in the form of memory or remorse or prescience or creation or pissing away a life, there is only here and only now—here at Broad and Girard, waiting for the #15 trolley that will take me to Corinthian Avenue, where I will see the ten-foot-high stone wall that surrounds the school, and will walk to the gatehouse and check in with the old guard, and wend my way back to the dormitory at Banker Hall or Merchant Hall or Mariner Hall, so yclept to memorialize the three professions of the school's founder, Stephen Girard, a Frenchman who became the richest man in America, director of the Second United States Bank, financier of the War of 1812, and who, childless, a stranger in a strange land, left those millions for "poor white male orphans."

Left all that money for me.

On campus, I pass the life-size marble statue of the benefactor at his sarcophagus in Founder's Hall, the most precise replica of the Parthenon in the world and a monument to Stephen Girard's psyche: the building he designed with minute specificity took years to complete, nearly frittered away his entire bequest, and had so many defects that it served little practical use other than to declare its own might and celebrate Pericles.

If Philadelphia was the Athens of America in the 1800s, Girard wanted to be its Pericles. Pericles ("surrounded by glory") was the golden boy in the Golden Age of Athens, the driving force for art and education, and the primary reason Athens is still known as the cultural center of ancient, democratic Greece. Pericles also oversaw the rebuilding of war-damaged structures on the Acropolis—including the Parthenon—in order to beautify the city, display its glory, and give work to the people.

Girard fancied himself Pericles.

Looking up at his statue from the main road, my benefactor appears to be anything but a Greek hero—he is an austere, short, bald, bushy-browed, one-eyed pirate in his Sunday go-to-meeting best, except he didn't go to any Sunday meetings because he was irreligious and worked on his fortune seven days a week. His demeanor was so cold that it repelled everyone it touched, except those for whom he made money. On no other level could this awkward foreign man compete in the capital of America, so he kept score with dollars.

The inscription under him reads: "My deeds must be my life. When I am dead, my actions must speak for me."

Every teacher and instructor quoted those lines. What an unintended benediction for a boy who wanted to be a writer. I could not hear or pass those words daily without meditating on their inherent contradiction: measly words speaking as clearly, carrying as much heft, as any of his deeds.

What we were not taught was that Negroes were instrumental in making our benefactor a wealthy man back in 1790 when he had two ships in the port of Haiti (then known as Saint-Domingue). When the slave revolt erupted, wealthy white planters hid their treasures on Girard's ships for safekeeping. The rich families were subsequently murdered and Captain Girard floated away with the collective bounty, estimated to be between $50,000 and $500,000.

Merci beaucoup, esclaves du Haïti.

Girard knew what to do with lucre.

What we were not taught was that once Stephen Girard settled in Philadelphia, and after he became a successful wine merchant and international mariner, he secretly sold arms to South American revolutionaries, including Simón Bolívar. When lending America money during the War of 1812, Girard, in a brilliant move, requested treasury notes in lieu of interest.

Merci beaucoup, Etats-Unis.

What we were not taught was that his wife, Mary, an independent sort, was housed in the lunatic asylum at Pennsylvania Hospital for twenty-five years, and inspired a play, a century later, called *The In-*

sanity of Mary Girard, which suggested that she had been driven mad by a domineering, powerful husband and a primitive mental health system. Thanks for nothing.

What we were not taught was that Girard owned slaves, took two mistresses, and was known far and wide as a miser, a taskmaster, a sourpuss, and defiantly indifferent to the English language. If being the richest man in America is tough to pull off in proper Quaker society when you have had a Catholic upbringing and proclaim agnosticism, when your ships are named *Rousseau, Voltaire, Montesquieu,* and *Helvetius,* when you are uncomfortable in your own skin, when you have a disfigured phyz due to the loss of an eye in childhood, then best to become a local hero. During the yellow fever epidemic of 1798, Girard organized an emergency committee at a hospital and then ran the place himself when it desperately needed a man in charge. In the midst of the scourge that took five thousand lives, Girard worked tirelessly and generously. He was finally loved. Until the reading of his will.

When I entered the school at seven years old, I was considered a newbie Hummer. Ever since a young boy with a foreign accent looked around and said, "This is my new hum," students were called Hummers. You could live for twelve years at Girard without ever seeing actual money. Room, board, clothing, medicine, dentistry, and education were free. Among the 1,200 students, there were six other Jews.

My first night at nonsectarian Girard, a prayer was said at dinner that ended with "In Jesus' name, Amen." At bedtime, we knelt by our metal cots and said the Lord's Prayer in unison. The governess told me I had 'til the end of the week to memorize Psalms 23 and 100. There were thirty-five cots in my dorm, separated by metal lockers where boys kept clothing and any earthly possessions. Freshly laundered clothes, underwear, socks, and two clean shirts, arrived three times a week, Monday, Wednesday, and Friday. We wore ties and jackets to school every day, knit vests when the weather turned bad. We marched everywhere in single or double file, alphabetical order.

All meals were silent. Baked scrod was served with spinach my second night at Girard. I could not stomach spinach. I left it on my plate.
A governess noticed the wet green mound and insisted I give it a try. I
soldiered onward. I vomited on the table. The entire third grade had
to run laps around the playground when dinner was over because of
my alimentary episode.

We went to the chapel on campus Wednesday morning and then
again Sunday morning, as we would for the next decade. The huge
Grecian cathedral was the largest house of worship I had ever seen,
and the brightest; our synagogue in Logan was tiny and dingy. I
thought God had an aversion to bright light. This chapel seated 2,400
people under its ninety-foot-high gold-leaf ceiling. It had stone
columns, towering stained glass windows, and an organ with over one
hundred stops and more than six thousand pipes. Over the years, in
that chapel, I would sing hymns in the choir and carols at Christmas
concerts, and pray to Jesus Christ, Lord and Savior.

That first Friday night, we went to Vespers. I had no idea what Vespers were. Even today, I am unsure—something vaguely Catholic, or
ecclesiastical, a service of worship held in the evening. Sermons were
followed by a movie. We saw lots of horror movies at Girard. We
laughed at them. The Creature from the Black Lagoon would be
mincemeat in our school. I was seated between two older boys. When
the lights went down and the movie went on, I felt hands on my
penis. No words were spoken. Soon, the two boys led my hands to
their penises. I had never felt another boy's penis before, and no one
had ever touched mine. I can't recall if I ever touched my own in such
a lambent manner, being only seven and all. The two penises were
large and smooth and tumescent and different, one from another, one
straight and skinny, and the other fatter with an extra flap of skin. All
this touching and being touched was strange, but not unpleasant. I
looked around. No one paid any attention. *The Creature from the
Black Lagoon* was more captivating. All of this was done so matter-of-
factly, so nonchalantly, the unbuttoning of my fly, the repositioning of

my fingers, that I could only assume it was a time-honored practice in this school, in this new place where I would live.

Unable to discern if this was an ordinary initiation rite or an ugly hazing, I went along quietly with that unresolved duality. I was in a world where I didn't know right from wrong. You'd think I would have, but I didn't. I was a Newbie.

I remember the boys' names to this day, and they remember mine; the uncircumsized boy was thrown out of Girard within a couple years for failing grades and misbehaving; the other graduated with me ten years later. I had more sex my first year at Girard College than I did my first year at Temple University. That's what I wrote in a piece I did for *Philadelphia* magazine a little while back: *I had more sex my first year at Girard College than I did my first year at Temple University.*

A letter was sent to the editor of the magazine. It read:

"As part of full disclosure, I must say that I knew this author when he was a student at Girard College, when I was a member of the house staff when he was a senior at that school. I was later the resident psychologist there.

"It is with that background that I took particular notice of his comments about that school, particularly when he wrote something to the effect that he had more sex when he was a seven-year-old boy at Girard than he did at Temple University. . . .

"It is very easy to cast aspersions on staff members, surely all long since dead, for not properly protecting this boy from abuse by other staff members or perhaps fellow students. His reference could be clearer and so the work of this 'terrific writer' (your term) could have been improved. Or perhaps he was the perpetrator of unspecified sexual activities.

"If it is the former and he has allegations against the school, perhaps it would be well for him to consider filing suit to seek compensation for damages he might have suffered. Despite the long time since he was seven, surely some lawyer will find a way to deal with this potential case. With victory, that money may go a long way to help him to get help in handling what might appear to be unresolved or unforgiven harsh views of his parents. . . .

"If he were the perpetrator, it might also be worth further study as to what was the source of such behavior, not expected from a seven-year-old boy in those days. Again, Bruce might benefit from discovering this."

The letter, unpublished, was passed along to me. I answered it thusly:

Dear Mr. Trevanian,

So nice to hear from you for the second time in all these years. The last time, you attacked me for making a reference to Uncle Eddie Savitz, the man who lured more than five thousand boys into his apartment for sex and the collection of their underwear and feces, and who infected untold numbers of them with AIDS. You defended Uncle Eddie and reproached my morality.

Here you are again, these many years later, still reading a long article and focusing on a solitary sentence, and condemning the victim (me) and then accusing him (me) of taking a cowardly shot at your colleagues. That the housemasters did not, or could not, protect any young boys (me) is one possibility that you raise, and then accuse the author (me) for not going into more detail. You want details? Names of boys and particulars of their acts? You want to know where we did it and what we did and how it went down in the lavatories and fire escapes, at the Friday night movies and in the dorms? The author (me) thought it wiser to leave out those prurient details. One (me) can only imagine how you would have reacted had the author (me) been graphic.

Here, then, is the long-winded if expurgated version of what you wanted. The Girard College I attended in the 1950s was a hotbed of sexuality and everyone knew it, students and staff alike. You lock up one thousand boys who are approaching or have arrived at puberty, and only a fool would have thought oth-

erwise. That no professional knew how to deal with this quotidian phenomenon was a sad matter, though not uncommon in most institutions—same-sex or coed. Your unabated harassment of the "victim" (me) may be considered by some as rather sadistic. Hell, even the Catholic Church apologizes for acts perpetrated and covered up twenty years ago, or a hundred years ago. You cannot even find that small gesture in your heart.

It is typical in the culture of abuse. Attack the victims. Keep them quiet. Don't talk about the transgressions, the suffering, the mistakes, the aftermaths. Don't permit any discussion during the abusive period or any time thereafter. Never is the only acceptable time. And then accuse the speaker of speaking ill of the dead, as if it would have been kinder of me to tell my tale while the teachers and housemasters were still alive, and to name their names. You would not have sanctioned that. God knows, the only permissible action is no action at all. Silence is golden in the land of disturbance.

I am no longer silent, Mr. Trevanian, and you are not dead. You are still blaming the victim (me). Why not? That always worked at Girard College. But we are in the larger world now, not a cloistered forty-four acres where you make the rules and mete out the punishment. It must be as difficult to break free from that culture for you as it is for me. Fifty years later, you are still insinuating that it was a seven-year-old boy who initiated sexual liaisons with others, with boys twice his age, or staff members twice their age.

I was never sexually abused by a staff member, if you don't count corporal punishment. In fifth grade, I was paddled every few nights by the white-haired governess in Section 10. My infractions ranged from loitering to imperfect hospital corners to smiling at the wrong time. Before lights out, she made me kneel beside a bed as if to pray, raise my nightshirt, and then she would whack me. Usually ten times. And then she would tell me to go to sleep. It was her little psychosexual-S&M dance. I was nine.

I was spanked with Ping-Pong paddles and sawed-off oars, with bamboo poles and hard, flat items of unknown origin. I was paddled by housemasters and swimming instructors and English teachers and governesses and other boys. One housemaster would hand a boy the paddle and say, "You do it, or I will. And I am a helluva lot stronger and meaner than either of you." As a favor to each other, the boys walloped each other in front of the rest of the class. Pants down, dignity too.

So you were the school psychologist after I graduated. Sweet Jesus, where is your empathy, Mr. Trevanian? Is this how you listened to the boys who came to you for comfort and compassion? I was a senior when you arrived. You were the Newbie. You came from seminary school, as I recall, and were a quiet, decent man, eager to learn how the school operated. You learned all too well.

Sincerely yours,
Bruce Buschel
Class of '63

9

DON'T SHRED THE LETTUCE

Poplar Street to Vine Street

N ORTH Broad is dirty with three types of chains—fast food, gas stations, and pharmacies. At Broad and Poplar, a McDonald's Drive Thru is connected to an Amoco station. Soon enough, someone will link the three chains into one full self-service pharmagaseteria—fill your tank, your belly, and your arteries: two burgers, large fries, two Prevacids, one Lipitor, and a liter of diet water to wash it all down.

The rest of the block, from Poplar to Parrish, is totally gone. Don't ask where. Just gone. Flattened like Fallujah. Only there were no insurgents or freedom fighters here. Only families. Philadelphians. Gone.

When the price of gasoline goes higher, the pharmagaseterias will have to incorporate the fourth most popular business on Broad Street: check-cashing joints. Of the ten establishments on Broad Street, three of the biggest are owned by United. Like this one at Fairmount Avenue.

"We are more secure than any bank," says Big Jim Higgins, director of marketing for United Financial Services. "We have bullet-resistant glass, mantraps, alarms, and some things I cannot tell you."

"What things?"

"I cannot tell you."

What Big Jim Higgins wants to talk about are the wonderful services offered by United, since critics accuse check cashers of preying on the poor and shylocking the shy.

"We don't keep banker's hours. We're available and we give instant money."

"You give money?"

"You don't have to wait for your check to clear. We assess the risk and we front the money."

The money fronted by United was already earned by the consumer and taxed by the government. While United has other services—money orders, money wiring, phone cards, and the like—85 percent of its business is cashing checks and 85 percent of those are payroll checks. Some risk.

"Our clientele has unsophisticated needs," says Big Jim. "They are transient people in service-related fields, waitress, janitor, hotel maid, gas station attendant. Most of the them have bank accounts, but still prefer our services."

"Why?" I ask.

"They may not have the money to cover their paycheck or they may not have a checking account. We help them out."

"Why don't they have a checking account?"

"They may not write enough checks to make it worthwhile. Or can't keep the minimum balance required. They may not have a bank account at all."

"Why don't they have a bank account?"

"Millions of consumers prefer to manage their money on a cash basis, so we buy the check after assessing the risk and then we are responsible for collecting the value of the check we purchased."

"How much do you charge?"

"It depends on the instant risk assessment. Between one and two percent. On average, 1.8 percent of the check."

"How much for a personal check?"

"We rarely accept personal checks."

"How many checks actually bounce?"

"Our bounce rate is one tenth of one percent."

Last year, United grossed $1.3 billion from 140 franchises in seventeen states. Business has doubled in the last decade. There are twenty-three United outlets in Philly and more on the way. Broad Street is good, but the suburbs are better. As long as immigration keeps growing, so will United.

So far today, over the course of seven miles, I have seen no skateboarders, no skaters, one bicyclist, and one motorcyclist, a cop on a Harley-Davidson Road King. And now my first jogger. You know you are getting near Center City when you see a jogger. At Broad and Mt. Vernon; the jogger has a dalmatian. See Spot jog. Spot doesn't dig jogging. It prevents him from chasing rats and real estate speculators. EB Realty is converting this city block into modern apartments. EB Realty is busy, with places from the Main Line to South Street. One of EB's strategies is to include ample parking, even when near Center City; Philadelphians love their cars. Another EB Realty trademark is signature names that are simultaneously hip and historic: Marine Club, Cigar Factory Condos, Divine Lorraine.

What will 640 North Broad be called?

"No name yet," says a South Philly boy who has quite a name himself: Anura Karthink Vivekananthan. Kar, as he is called, is VP of EB Development. He is expansive about parking and security and history: this building once housed Mulford Pharmaceutical, which, back in 1925, produced a diphtheria serum that saved countless Eskimos from certain death when diphtheria, a white man's disease for which the natives had no natural immunity, swept across a region of Alaska. The serum traveled from 640 Broad Street to Seattle, Washington, by rail and then to the last train stop in Nenana, Alaska. But how to get it to the villages? After small planes were ruled out because 40 degrees below would kill the antitoxins, twenty drivers (Russian, Irish, Norwegian, native) and one hundred huskies were hooked up to dogsleds that traversed nearly seven hundred miles from Nenana to Nome.

That rescue journey is commemorated to this day by the Iditarod Trail Sled Dog Race. "Iditarod" means either "clean water" or "distant place," depending on your source.

"Why not call it Iditarod Apartments?" I ask.

"Oh no," says Kar. "Some dog lovers hate that race."

"How come?"

"Cruel to the animals. We would rather avoid any controversy."

"Will you allow dogs at 640 North Broad?" I ask.

"Oh no, no dogs allowed," says Kar.

"That's a catchy name."

"What's that?" asks Kar.

"No Dogs Allowed."

"I'll take it under advisement," says Karthink Vivekananthan.

(Rule #19 of the Iditarod Race is called "Expired Dogs" and reads thusly: "Any dog that expires on the trail must be taken by the musher to a checkpoint. The musher may transport the dog to either the checkpoint just passed or the upcoming checkpoint. An expired dog report must be completed by the musher and presented to a race official along with the dog. . . . The musher is withdrawn or disqualified unless the cause of death is an external force beyond the musher's control such as a moose or snow machine.")

Having walked now about eight miles, I don't recall any dog droppings or people with pooper-scoopers. The streets have been relatively clean. Not scrubbed like Amsterdam, but neat. If there is a smell that permeates Broad Street, it's the muted odor of fried onions, for every cuisine, every food shop, every diner, every truck, everyone uses fried onions. Except the tall thin gent in the black suit, white shirt, and red bow tie selling bean pies for $6 in the middle of NoBro near Cumberland Street. He is from Mohammad's Mosque #12, Nation of

Islam. (There are one mosque and one synagogue, Rodeph Shalom, and thirty-four churches on Broad Street.)

Here's his bean pie recipe:

- Cook 2 cups navy beans until soft.
- Preheat oven to 350°.
- In blender, put beans, 4 eggs, 1 stick butter, one 14 oz. can evaporated milk, 2 teaspoons flour, 1 teaspoon nutmeg. Mix at medium speed for 2 minutes.
- Add 2 cups sugar and 2 teaspoons vanilla. Mix well.
- Pour into favorite pie shells. Bake 1 hour, until golden brown. Makes 2 or 3 pies depending on size of shells. Five minutes after removing from oven, cover with plastic wrap that clings.
- When cooled down, either eat or sell on Broad Street.

Under construction at 410 North Broad is the future administrative headquarters for the school district. Retail stores will open, Starbucks and Banana Republic. Maybe a Philly Soft Pretzel Factory. Restaurants will follow suit. As of yet, the famous "restaurant renaissance" has not found its way north of City Hall. Maybe Stephen Starr, great American restaurateur and owner of a dozen plush places in town, will expand his empire to NoBro. And then I can take Tom Ferrick Jr. there for a nice dinner.

Next to the construction site is the Inquirer Building, a stately white edifice that speaks more to character than adventure, as reflected in the staid newspaper produced therein. I stop to see Tom Ferrick Jr. I don't really want to see Tom Ferrick Jr. Nothing personal, but if he looks great, I'll feel bad. If he looks bad, I'll feel terrible. I don't trust his photo in the newspaper. Newspapers lie. I used to work at newspapers. At the *Inquirer*, truth be told. At my interview with legendary editor Gene Roberts—under whose leadership the *Inquirer* won seventeen Pulitzers between 1975 and 1990, more than any paper in the nation— he asked me to name my favorite writer. Vladimir Nabokov, I said. He stared at me as if I were speaking a foreign language. He asked for suggestions to improve the Sunday magazine. I polished off a few pearls about investigatory vigor and fearless "new journalism" and, when given a choice, to always take the literary high road. He reminded me that my last story started in Carol Miller's bedroom and then turned really raunchy. Carol Miller was a rock 'n' roll DJ with a sexy voice and lots of yellow hair. I wonder what she's doing today. I bet she took good care of herself. Maybe reunions aren't half bad after all.

Who am I kidding? I hate reunions. I can't even go to CSN concerts, or C&N concerts, or CSNY concerts, or Y concerts. I get depressed watching other people's reunions, let alone my own. I don't need reminders of yesterday. I need blinders. I know the past was better than the present before I begin. I knew that the moment my sons left home. And I know the future will be rife with frustrations and a fading tennis game and global warming and metastasizing sorrows and a less-than-grand finale at Goldstein Rosenberg Raphael-Sacks Inc. Prone to remorse, seeing a college buddy will only remind me of unfulfilled potentials. Mine, not his. Aside from my sons, beautiful in every way, what I will leave this world is negligible.

Now, does ol' Tom Ferrick Jr. need me to tell him that things don't turn out the way you planned?

The guard in the lobby at 400 NoBro dials Ferrick's private number. It's his voicemail. Relieved, I leave a warm message and walk out. What if I run into ol' Tom right now, in the doorway of the lobby? Gulp. The one person I know I will not see at the *Inquirer* is perhaps the most famous member of the *Inquirer,* Stephen A. Smith. He certainly has no time or inclination to write a column at the office when there is so much radio and television time to fill on ESPN.

Stephen A. Smith is single-handedly, emblematically, putting newspapers out of business. The only reason to read a newspaper when you can see the video clips on your computer and hear interviews on the radio is if the column brings something unique and penetrating, if the words on the paper are selected and arranged in an order that will offer something unavailable from other media. Insight. Outrage. Sagacity. Newspapers are so slow, so still, so yesterday that writers have to, now more than ever, work at their craft, create a style, or transfer their own personality onto the page. They have to go places cameras cannot, behind the scenes, inside the psyches. Stephen A. Smith just talks. And talks. And loves to hear himself talk. Half the words that flow like a waterfall from his mouth are unnecessary and unenlightening and would be excised by a decent editor. Stephen A. Smith doesn't have one. He has cameras and microphones. He uses his publication for street cred, for health insurance, for a prestigious line in his bio. He must spend more time in makeup than at a keyboard. Where could anyone find enough hours in a day to devote two of those hours to live radio, another one to a sixty-minute television show, parts of hours to special reports on *NBA Shootaround*, attend practices, eat meals, interview players, call general managers, read salient features, see a live sporting event, take a leak, visit a post-game locker room, watch other games on satellite, check the ratings with Arbitron and Nielsen, and then sit down and write 750 words that have to be considered, written, pondered, rewritten, scrambled, unscrambled, edited, rewritten, and have them turn into an eminently readable column?

The best-known newspaper writer in Philadelphia is killing newspapers.

Race Street, counterintuitively, has nothing to do with family lineage, genetics, and color. Originally called Sassafras Street, it became so identified with horse racing that its name was changed to Race Street in 1853 so people could find it more easily and not miss the first few races while wandering about the city asking for directions.

On the corner of Race Street is a Quiznos subs. Quiznos either has a bad research department or big balls. Your average gambler would have to bet against a sub chain making it in a hoagie town. Hoagies are imprinted on young Philadelphians like Mother Goose on goslings.

Quiznos? It's a chain that started somewhere in Denver, Colorado, and has three thousand stores in fifteen countries and 200 million dollars' worth of bragging rights. What kind of hoagie do they serve in Kuwait or Bahrain? What do they substitute for the cappicola? I stand and watch the people entering or exiting Quiznos. They are a cut above the people who enter and exit Subway. It is obvious from casual observation that they are vulnerable to advertising, possess thousands of damaged papillae, or had a misguided upbringing. If only they had tasted a Lee's Hoagie before this degenerate habit took hold. The Hoagie Supreme from Lee's Hoagies has been the template for every sandwich I have ever concocted or dreamed about. Once you master cheesesteaks and hoagies, all other sandwiches—paninis, Cubans, BLTs, grilled cheeses, and grinders—are child's play. The day I got my driver's license, my second stop, after picking up all the guys at the candy store, was Lee's Hoagies on Cheltenham Avenue. A Supreme, potato chips, Frank's black cherry wishniak, and a *Daily News*. That was heaven in the afternoon. Quiznos is the other place.

While on the topic, here is the best recipe I know for a hoagie:

- Cut the roll—never separate the two halves—remove excess bread.
- Three squirts of soy oil from a plastic squirt bottle will moisten the roll.
- Lay down a bed of iceberg lettuce—never shredded.
- Crisscross slices of provolone cheese across both sides of roll.
- Add four slices cotechino, five slices cappicola, six slices Genoa salami, five thinly sliced Jersey tomatoes, and thinly sliced white onions to taste.
- Add some peppers in oil.
- Three more squirts of soy oil.
- Add a generous amount of freshly chopped oregano, ground pepper, and salt.

- Use a large knife to hold contents in place whilst refolding the two halves back together.
- *Mangiare!*

Between Race and Vine is Hahnemann Hospital, or what used to be Hahnemann Hospital until it became Allegheny Medical College of Pennsylvania/Hahnemann School of Medicine and went bankrupt and was sold to the Tenet Healthcare Corporation but managed by Drexel University and now goes by the exaltation HUH (Hahnemann University Hospital) and sometimes THUD (Tenet Hahnemann University Drexel). This was the first homeopathic hospital in America, named for the father of homeopathy, Dr. Samuel Hahnemann. You will find no homeopathy practiced here today and hardly a physician or nurse who would recommend it, endorse it, or even know what the hahnemann you are talking about.

I enter Dr. Sam's Place this fine day for the sole purpose of using its lavatory facilities. Everyone has more important things to do than look for strangers who micturate. In New York, you can rarely enter a building taller than five stories without being carded, checked out, identified, and followed by cameras. Philadelphia is lax by comparison, and the hospitals strange in their security measures. Not once in the hundred visits to my mother in any hospital, ER, ICU, psych ward, or rehab center did anyone ever ask for an ID or proof of my relation to the patient. Walk right in. Yet, on the phone, every nurse turned into a secret agent: "I cannot give out any information about your alleged mother over the phone."

"I swear I'm her son," I would say. "How is she doing?"

"I'd like to help you, but I don't want to lose my license," the nurse would say.

"But I can help you," I would say.

"How's that?"

"I know the patient intimately. She takes Lanoxin .25 mg for atrial fib, prednisone 30 mg for her extreme psoriasis, a beta-blocker for blood pressure, Lasix for heart failure, Prilosec for an ulcer, Effexor 100 mg and Prozac 20 mg for depression, slow-release iron for anemia, a variety of laxatives to combat the iron, hot coffee all day long, and Winston Lights on demand."

"Hold on, please . . ."

I would hold.

"Hello, this is Dr. So-and-So."

"Hello, I am calling about my mother, Rose Buschel."

The doctors were usually kind and polite. One time, a doctor got on the phone and said, "Your mother has broken her neck."

"What?"

"She fell and she broke her neck."

"How is she doing?"

"Not good. We put her in a comatose state so she doesn't move. If she moves, there is a real danger it could affect other things, rub against the spinal column, inflict serious paralysis."

"My God."

"We have some important decisions to make. There are a few ways to go."

"Surgery?" I asked.

"A possibility. But her age makes that complicated. The neuro people and the spinal people will be here tomorrow morning at 7 A.M. They will confer and then we'll have some better answers."

"Can I be there?"

"I suppose so."

I call my brother and other relatives. I drive to Philadelphia. It is a very long night.

I walk into my mother's room in Intensive Care at 7 A.M. She is alone, except for the machinery and screens with green LED numbers and waves. A tube is down her throat, white adhesive tape prevents her face from moving, her eyes too are taped shut, her hands and feet are tethered to the bed. Sustenance flows through the IV. A machine helps her breathe. My first reaction is to the primitive nature of the setup: tubes and adhesive tape and leather shackles. This could be 1915, the year she was born. Or 1815.

I wipe her brow, she does not react. Not to my touch or my weeping. She looks terrible. Worse than ever. In the past, reports from doctors or anecdotes from companions or even her voice on the phone made her sound worse than the reality of seeing her; not that there hadn't been changes, notable deteriorations, but her essence was always luminous, her anger persistently front and center, and she was always rather cute. Today she looks worse than anything I imagined. She looks almost dead. Is this how she will look in the casket? Would that be preferable to what lies ahead for her? Paralysis. Pain. Indignity. Should I pray for her recovery or her departure from this mortal coil?

At eight o'clock, the doctor on duty shows up.

"Hello," I say.

"She doesn't have a broken neck," he says.

"What?"

"The technician who read the X-rays last night, he's not that good, we don't really trust him. The expert came in this morning and reread the X-rays, and he guarantees me she doesn't have a broken neck."

"What does she have?"

"Nothing, as far as we can tell."

"Nothing?"

"There was something on the film, a smudge, or a sign of osteoporosis, but nothing's broken."

"You don't trust the guy who read the X-rays last night, but you put my mother in a coma and told me her neck was broken."

"Aren't you happy to hear she doesn't have a broken neck?"

"Well, yes, but . . . look at her . . . she's doped up, and tied down."

"I thought you'd be happy to hear the good news."

"Maybe I should be happy, doc, but what I'm really feeling is that I'd like to break your fucking neck. That might make me happy."

From the intubation, she didn't eat for a week. From the induced coma, she didn't walk for a week. She hadn't smoked, hadn't taken her antidepressants, hadn't eaten or evacuated, and had lost weight she could ill afford losing. All this set her back immeasurably. She was really never the same.

When she could talk again, she got right to the point.

"I can't do this anymore," she said.

"I know, Mom, I know."

"Get me a gun," she said.

"How about a full-time nurse?"

"I would prefer a gun."

"You don't know how to use a gun, Mom."

"How hard can it be? Look at all the idiots who use guns."

"They're very heavy."

"Get me a gun. I'll show you how strong I am."

"If you are really serious about this, there are better ways, Mom."

"Tell me and I'll do it. Please."

"I'll call Lee in California and bring Ben from Seattle, and Josh, and Noah and Marin and Tina and your sister and her kids and your best friends and we'll all gather together for a great day or a weekend, and we'll say our goodbyes in warmth and love. How's that sound?"

"You mean you would bring all my children and grandchildren to Philadelphia?"

"Yes, Mom. We'll do it right. No child left behind."

"And they'd all be in my apartment at the same time?"

"Yes."

"But if I had all you there, why would I want to die?"

10

360 Degrees of Edmund Bacon

City Hall to Walnut Street

I approach City Hall and its nine hundred rooms, twenty elevators, eighty-eight million bricks, and four clock faces bigger than London's Big Ben. The celebrated structure upon which William Penn stands took an absurd thirty years to build, from 1871 to 1901, and was the national symbol of municipal corruption and incompetence.

Philadelphia politics. You will not soon see a woman running for mayor. Philadelphia is a masculine town. Nothing feminine about the place. Not physically, historically, artistically, or spiritually. Even the highest-ranking female official, DA Lynne Abraham, is as studly as they come. Called "the deadliest DA" by *The New York Times,* she has sought the death penalty in 85 percent of her murder cases.

Philadelphia politics. They say the only sure things around here are race and taxes, and taxes can be finagled. John Street, African-American Democrat, garnered 98 percent of the black vote. Sam Katz, Caucasian-American Republican, won 80 percent of the white vote. Philadelphia politics. Oh, City of Brotherly Love. Where a onetime street vendor named Street bestrides the city. Where a mayor named Goode fire-bombed the city. Where a mayor named Rizzo—"I make bristle" in Italian—set a standard for corruption and cronyism so high, or low, that no one bristles at minor-league scams and stray Molotov cocktails.

There are over a million eligible voters in Philadelphia. Not half that number voted in the mayoral election. In America, citizens have the right to not vote and politicians have the opportunity to steal votes and erase votes and create votes where none existed. If the politicians get caught, the citizens have the right to punish them. Having all these rights can be great fun and a real headache.

The last time I was in City Hall, it was to learn valuable lessons about the politics of jurisprudence and journalism. I was the editor of the *Drummer,* a weekly alternative newspaper in the 1970s, when a columnist wrote about taking a date to Mexico City for the first International Women's Conference. His date happened to be the feminist writer for the *Inquirer.* A funny piece, it parodied the women's movement by turning everything on its ear, from female cabbies to male strip clubs. The columnist somehow ended up at the head table, where, during a speech by Gloria Steinem, someone unzipped him under the table and jerked him off. As he climaxed, he turned to Betty Friedan, mother of all feminists, who said, with a Cheshire Cat grin, "Girls will be girls."

"Is this true?" I asked the columnist.

"Not a word of it," he said.

"Did you go to Mexico City?"

"Why would I go there? Too many feminists."

"Might we get sued?" I asked.

"Not a chance," he said. "I am friendly with everyone in the piece and they all have a sense of humor. You have my word."

I called Betty Friedan, just in case, and she was indeed good-natured. "If only I had the time for such activities," she said.

So I ran the column. We were sued. By the feminist writer for the *Inquirer.* And she used her paper's powerhouse law firm, the kind with five names, each more WASPy than the last.

"Might we have to go to court?" I asked my columnist.

"Not a chance," he said.

"She said your column raped her in print," I said. "You made her feel dirty and disgusting."

"She's very dramatic," he said, "but this won't go to court."

"How can you be so sure?" I asked.

"No newspaper would ever sue another newspaper for a satire."

The first week in court was a roller coaster. After expert testimony from noted satirists, including P. J. O'Rourke, then at the *National Lampoon,* the judge ruled that the column was in fact satirical, but insisted it still possessed the power to defame.

Our team was stumped. Since the owner of the *Drummer* and his columnist had much to lose—money and standing—and I had none of either, I suspected they were preparing me to take the fall. I told the judge of my suspicions. He did not disagree. I told him I wanted to defend myself. He disagreed vehemently, telling me his courtroom was not a carnival, and demanding that I return Monday morning with my own unclownish attorney. I found one in the legal Yellow Pages, an ex-Marine boxer who had never been to court on a libel or defamation case. He was young and eager and cheap and tough as nails. I liked him just fine.

During the next week, the settlement money demanded by the plaintiff shot up and down like a hot stock, depending on the day's testimony. Even as the jury deliberated, if I agreed to pay her $25,000, I could walk. The columnist and the publisher would pay more. But I didn't feel guilty of anything, I told my attorney, and I didn't have $25,000. He stared at me for the briefest moment, then threw me up against the wall in the corridor of City Hall, lifting me off my feet, and yelled into my eyeballs, "This is not about guilt or innocence. Grow up, hippie-dippie. The only people who don't lose money here today are the lawyers and the judge. The rest of you lose. The only thing yet to be determined is how much you lose. Pay her $25,000 and consider it a bargain. She wants a half million bucks.

Don't be a fool. And don't talk about guilt or innocence. No one cares."

My faith in journalism and instant karma and America and Learned Hand and all that had a slim chance of being right with the world on the line. Like a fool, I turned down the offer.

The jury levied punitive damages against the columnist of $55,000 and $75,000 more against the newspaper. The compensatory damages were another $5,000. At the time, it was the largest verdict ever awarded in a Pennsylvania libel case.

I walked. Scot-free.

Okay, occasionally, bloody infrequently, something works out the way you planned it.

Today, I arrive at City Hall around the same time as do a hundred angry workers, four television camera crews, two hovering helicopters, and numerous police on foot and horseback. The plainclothes cops are as easy to spot as the uniformed ones. District Council #33 is pissed. It is the blue-collar wing of the State, County and Municipal Workers. Their brother union, #47, the white-collar wing, has already made a sweet deal with the city after discovering a "secret" $2.8 million in its health care fund. Directed by leaders with bullhorns, Local #33 members are marching past the exact spot where Mummers get judged and win prizes on New Year's Day. No one is wearing feathers today or carrying a banjo. They are singing songs and carrying signs: "No Contract, No Peace." "The City Works Because We Do."

Philly is a union town, always has been. The carpenters who built Carpenter's Hall in 1770 went out on strike in 1797. It is a working-class city with an underdog's mentality, and the collar around the dog's neck is blue. Having once been the center for industry and railroads, unions have long been an essential part of Philly life; having lost most of its industry and its status, Philadelphians carry around a chip on their shoulders so large it requires scaffolding. You need union guys for that.

Ever since Ronald Reagan fired all the striking air traffic controllers in 1980 and never rehired a single one, unions have fallen on hard times. But Philadelphia public school employees have gone on strike five times since 1965. Public transit went on strike for forty days in the summer of 1998 and then again in the winter of 2005. A half million people were denied the buses, subways, trolleys, and elevated trains. No citizen enjoys the inconvenience of a strike, but Philadelphians consider it an inevitable part of life. As Ben Franklin said, or should have said: no man who works for another man can be overpaid.

If you are a drinking man, seeing the number 33 on so many high-flying banners and placards reminds you of Rolling Rock beer. Some saloon historians believe it represents the year Prohibition ended, or the number of words in the company credo on the bottle, or the lowest degree at which liquid will not freeze and beer is best consumed. Others firmly believe that the mysterious 33 on the Rolling Rock bottle celebrates the union that worked at the brewery in Latrobe.

Union leaders are currently negotiating with city officials—right in the middle of the street just to the north of City Hall. Billy Penn is peeking from on high. Pete Mathews, president of Local 33, recently called Mayor John Street a "gutless pig" and refuses to recant. I always thought pigs had guts, and you can probably find them in scrapple. I want more scrapple.

What an unexpected thrill this is, watching a union take to the streets, fomenting public sentiment, exercising their right to assemble, to throw around some weight, to march shoulder to shoulder, singing songs, carrying signs, men and women, black and white and brown, Americans all. Parents should bring their children to see this spectacle; more rousing by far than the Act One climax of *Les Mis*. And you leave this street theater humming their tune:

> We are the union
> the mighty mighty union
> everywhere we go

people want to know
who we are
so we tell them—
we are the union
the mighty mighty union
everywhere we go
people want to know
who we are
so we tell them—

Of all the sounds in the world, a chorus of men's voices raised in unison and gusto is one of the most stirring and chill producing; add female voices and car horns and screaming pedestrians and the clippety-clop of police horses and the staccato whir of helicopter blades, and you have yourself one fine urban symphony that you'd like to toast. And when they start marching, marching right at you, you better get out of the way.

To avoid the mounted police, I station myself behind the granite base of a bronze statue. It has been here since 1894. I am looking at four horse hooves on the ground, so I know the rider survived the depicted battle; according to sculpture protocol, one foot off means the rider was killed; two hooves in the air signifies a wounded rider. I look up and behold a pale horse: and his name that sat on him was Major General George McClellan. It's Little Mac, the big jerk. For whom surviving battles was rather easy—he avoided them, resisting sound strategy and presidential prodding. He too was a Union man. Different union, different march. He must be facing north because he was afraid to face the South. What is this guy doing here? Where is the blood on his hands? He seems so upright, so secure. He was, in fact, the general who had Robert E. Lee outnumbered two to one at Antietam but, due to piss-poor tactics, could manage only a gory standoff in the single bloodiest day in U.S. history, 12,400 Union losses and 10,700 dead Confederates; worse, the next day, Little Mac let General

Lee's battered boys retreat across the Potomac River into good ol' Virginny when he should have demolished the depleted Southern troops and brought the war to an abrupt finish. Day after day, week after week, Little Mac refused to attack, claiming the enemy had him outmanned when all intelligence said the opposite was true. In truth, he loved his men, and their love for him, too much to kill them.

Commander in Chief Lincoln sent him instructions to attack. Little Mac refused. Lincoln sent him pep talks, as only Lincoln could. Little Mac refused to budge. Lincoln finally paid him a personal visit in Maryland and demanded the Napoleonic general attack the Rebs. No dice. So Little Mac, all five foot three of him, was relieved of his duty, sent packing, and rode into the history books as the man who prolonged the Civil War for an unnecessary two, maybe three years. Historians are convinced that he was irrational to the brink of paranoia. His colleagues decided he was either a coward or a traitor.

You want worse? He ran for president against Lincoln in 1864 because he was against the Emancipation Proclamation.

What is he doing here, next to City Hall? What would the brothers of the City of Brotherly Love do if they knew? Who would blame them if they put a noose around this dude and toppled him like a Saddam Hussein monument? He is here only because he was born in Philly, went to West Point at sixteen, and his daddy cofounded Jefferson Medical Hospital. If there were a more well-known or more deserving local combatant from the Civil War, Little Mac would be gone.

You want worse? After failing to defeat Lincoln, he became the governor of New Jersey. Yes, the governor of New Jersey is astride a mighty steed at City Hall. Every Philadelphian knows New Jersey exists for three reasons: beaches and boardwalks in the scorching summers, Bruce Springsteen, and to make Philadelphians feel better about their situation since Jersey has a population denser than Japan's and suffers from more afflictions than the Old Testament. The Garden State is a double espresso in the afternoon for Philadelphians.

Every misbegotten city needs a state to look down on.

McClellan went to war on a horse and came home on foot. Not the military career he had mapped out. How ironic that his saddle is his lasting memorial. His saddle. The McClellan saddle. After West Point, he was sent to study the armies of Europe and observe the Crimean War. Impressed with Prussian and Hungarian cavalries, he recommended changes for the Army equestrian brigades. Cleverly contoured—one size fit all—his saddle was lightweight, handsome, durable, inexpensive, and a boffo success with the brass and cavalrymen. A wooden pommel was covered with rawhide, an open seat and a thick leather skirt, hickory or oak stirrups, girth strap made of woolen yarn, a blanket cushioning the saddle, and all hardware polished black varnish. It was standard issue for every branch of the Army, and the Marines, from 1859 until the cavalry was disbanded in 1942. And it is still used by the Mexican Army, Royal Canadian Mounted Police, and game wardens in South Africa, not to mention the officer from South Philadelphia who is asking me to move along so the union can continue its protest.

"You know what this general did in the war?" I ask.

"Looks like he rode a horse," says the officer.

"What kind of saddle you riding on?" I ask the policeman.

"Modified McClellan," he says. "Now move along."

"Yes sir, officer," I say, and move along, wondering why I spent so much time under this stupid statue anyway, when City Hall is surrounded by what amounts to an outdoor sculpture park.

(The Philly police have since shut down their equine division. Money is the reason given. There will be no more steeds in Center City and no more horseshit on Broad Street. Everything is getting cleaned up. It would be the Disneyfication of Broad Street if only Disney would deign to come to Philly. Alas, no mice, no horses. Much art.)

Within spitting distance of Little Mac is *Three Way Piece* by Henry Moore, a large Dubuffet, *Milord la Chamarre,* and Robert Engman's mighty *Triune.*

Jacques Lipchitz's *Government of the People* dominates the plaza directly across from City Hall. Human figures are piled high in an inverted pyramid, like a Pilobolus dance troupe sharing a bed, two on the bottom and then more on top and yet more bodies wrapping around each other, protecting each other, lifting each other. Democracy is messy.

From the first, it was dismissed by then mayor Frank Rizzo with a flippant "It looks like some plasterers dropped a load of plaster." Rizzo was apparently unaware that Lipchitz had turned Picasso's cubism into sculpture, had joined Brancusi and Moore (both represented within blocks of here) in the pantheon of twentieth-century sculptors, and had worked in Philly, loved Philly, and left Philly significant art along Kelly Drive, at the Barnes Foundation museum, and in front of the art museum, where his sleek *Prometheus Strangling the Vulture* stands guard against the philistines and unwashed mayoral critics.

The Lipchitz used to be alone on the plaza. Now it has company. Next to his immigrant's vision of democracy is a bulky, bronze, ten-foot statue of, wouldn't you know, Frank Rizzo. And the mayor still has his back turned toward the *Government of the People.*

And there's *Clothespin,* the Claes Oldenburg installation that altered the city's identity for many of its citizens. It was so gloriously hip, so anthropomorphically Pop, you wondered how the old-pol knuckleheads ratified a forty-five-foot-tall steel clothespin to stand in the shadow of City Hall, making the Beaux Arts mastodon seem more like a doll's house.

City Hall supports an entire megalopolis. A clothespin holds wet bedsheets on a line. Yang, meet yin.

When a cheap wooden household item, albeit a miracle of form and function, a gizmo simple enough to understand and clever enough to admire, is suddenly art, then so is your pencil, your pencil sharpener, your sled, your mittens, your Goldenberg Peanut Chew, a champagne cork, a manhole—everything had possibilities. And not just in your head, or in the hands of a foreign fop like Duchamp, but on the street where you live, where the subway stops. This was Philly's very own Campbell's soup can, family size.

As it was a reflection of, an homage to, Brancusi's *The Kiss,* which sits down the road, it started a conversation between the two couples. Such hard materials conveying such soft notions, making us hardheads such soft touches. The top parts of the *Clothespin* are faces staring at each other tenderly, slightly apart, ready for a kiss, their breasts and/or chests—genders are up for grabs—touching, and the arm of the stainless steel mechanism reaching around the merging bodies, belly to belly, hips to hips, and near the center, above the long legs, is the round hole of the mechanism that keeps it all together, that keeps the world going and populated, with its twisty spring where babies are conceived, where you were conceived, where a real person could actually curl up and sleep. This clothespin is not only your mother's favorite gizmo, it's your mother, and your father, standing there, hugging in the rain, in the sleet, baking in the sun, never apart. Having weathered gorgeously, rusted as if left behind from another eon, it's a wonder.

You walk around and through the *Clothespin* and then look up at William Penn. Built by Alexander Stirling Calder—father of sculptor Alexander Milne Calder, and grandfather of Alexander "Sandy" Calder, famous for his mobiles (so dubbed by Duchamp)—the twenty-six-ton, thirty-seven-foot replica of the Quaker Immigrant looks very different from this angle. Against an afternoon blue sky, his silhouette appears to have a long, thin erection, pointing toward North Philly, slightly downturned, but certainly delicate enough to blow in the wind.

Is it possible that the youngest Calder got the seed of the idea for metal moving in a breeze from staring up at grandpa's most famous statue? After all, little Alexander had his own studio as a child and was making sculptures at age twelve.

Did Penn's penis give creation to the first mobile?

Did Robert Indiana know what enmities his *LOVE* would generate? JFK Plaza was nicknamed Love Park with the arrival of his iconic image: the capital L and tilted O sitting on the stable V and E, a Pop painting that was transferred to stamps, posters, jewelry, and finally a red aluminum sculpture. Installed in 1976, when love was all you needed, when love was antiwar and pro-pot, not affection for flag, Mom, and Apple computers, the plaza was a great place to meet and be met. In the 1980s, it became a skateboarder's paradise, with its inviting schema of curved multitiered stairs, granite ledges and benches, marble surfaces, and long spaces. It became the setting for video games and magazine layouts, and was a major reason for Philly hosting the 2001 and 2002 X Games, luring a half million live spectators and 150 million eyeballs around the world. Skatadelphia! Subculture hot spot. Cooperstown of skateboarding. LOVE Park attracted Gen-Xers like the Haight did hippies in the 1960s, boards substituted for guitars, exercise for drugs, sweaty competition instead of free love. Stevie Williams, Anthony Pappalardo, and Ricky Oyola made their names, and fat bank accounts, in the multibillion-dollar skateboarding onslaught by being identified with LOVE Park's ledges and stair sets. Sweet, no?

No. Mayor John Street banned skateboarding at the park. Bang! Some say it was the luxury housing going up in the neighborhood, others say the hangout was becoming dangerous and lost its purpose of providing a public space in downtown urbania.

"Philly really messed up, man," Stevie Williams has said. "Cut off a lot of talent and cut off this avenue for success. John Street killed it. And now I feel bad, just for the fact that there's not going to be another me coming out of Philly. It sucks that I had to move. I'd give up all this shit to come back home and be able to skate LOVE, but I can't really afford not to skate, so I had to go."

Philly won't see Stevie Williams anytime soon. He earns a half million dollars a year from endorsements. He owns a mansion, his own clothing label, and a distribution company in Hollywood.

Williams was not the only person interested in reopening the park to boarders. DC Shoes, makers of Extreme sport apparel, offered the city $1 million for the maintenance, security, and upkeep. The offer was turned down.

And then a ninety-two-year-old gent protested the ban by skating in the park. Skating may be an overstatement. He coasted for a moment, with many helping hands, before dismounting and blasting the city. "I think it is very ungenerous of the city that it couldn't spare one of its 2,864 blocks for the skateboarders of the world. Show me a skateboarder who killed a little old lady and I'll reconsider." The civilly disobedient speaker/skater was Edmund Bacon, original designer of the space back in 1932 in a Cornell University thesis. It took him almost twenty years to become chief city planner and another fifteen before he got the plaza built, but Bacon was relentless. He was that rare amalgam of visionary and politician, able to see the future and get others to pay for it. Called the Father of Modern Philadelphia, he guided and chided, then wailed and admonished, and got developers to refurbish the city as he saw fit. Long after his two decades as city planner, he unhesitantly imposed his influence on the city of his birth, the city of his Quaker ancestors, the city he knew he would redesign since he stood atop City Hall as a kid and channeled William Penn and knew how Penn wanted the city to evolve and that he, little Eddie Bacon, had to become an architect to fulfill Penn's wishes. For the rest of his life, Bacon preached that any edifice that would climb higher than Penn would push the city's morals lower.

He was right. He knew architecture did more than provide shelter or line barons' pockets. It speaks viscerally to the citizenry and lets them know who and where they are. Billy Penn's lid kept the lid on things, kept the city in pleasing proportion, kept away the dark shadows of gothic skyscraper oppression. Edmund Bacon staved off the inevitable until 1987. Even today, however, there are only five buildings taller than Penn's 548-foot-high hat, which is not to say that all the architecture springs from a noticeably grand design, or delivers counterpoise, but the mixed use works; a tad cacophonous for some,

postmodern jazz for others. Any way you play it, you know you are
not in New York or Chicago. Philadelphians have a hard time ignor-
ing from whence they cometh or what is expected from them.

When he died in 2005 at the age of ninety-five, the obit headlines
were "Shaped U.S. Urban Renewal" and "Influenced a Generation of
City Planners" and "Renowned City Planner Transformed Postwar
Philadelphia." They would all end with "Bacon is survived by daughters Karin, Elinor, and Kira, and sons Michael, a musician, and Kevin,
an actor."

Ah, Kevin, an actor.

This fortunate nexus signals that place in this book where the author is meant to speak to the movie star, thereby sprinkling some glitter onto the city, and, more significantly, this project. Celebrity
power! Kevin Bacon has it. With no underbelly—no scandals, no arrests, no rehabs, just a hardworking actor who loves his wife (who
doesn't?), actress Kyra Sedgwick, and loves his kids, and cares about
Philadelphia and sings with his brother, Michael, and appears in underwear commercials, and inspired a parlor game to honor his pro-
lificacy, Six Degrees of Kevin Bacon. He has appeared in sixty movies
to date, and if he lives as long as his father, may be in another seventy-
five. And that doesn't count the movies he has or will direct.

(Other than Will Smith, Philly is really a tiny pond that has
spawned few big fish. Either they have already swum into the pages of
this book or they are only marginally associated with their birth
water: Maria Bello, Danny Bonaduce, Adam Carolla, Blythe Danner,
Kevin Eubanks, Richard Gere, Seth Green, Judith Jamison, Donald
Barthelme, Stanley Clarke, Jill Scott, Frankie Avalon, Eve, William
Wharton, Noam Chomsky.)

I call Kevin Bacon's agent. No money in interviews, so the agent
shuffles me along to his PR firm, PMK. Molly Schoneveld needs a
written request with the questions I intend to ask Mr. Bacon, so I
send Molly a written request with questions I intend to ask Mr.
Bacon, focusing on his father and his growing up in Philadelphia.

Molly wants to know how the release of this book can be tied to an upcoming Kevin Bacon project. I suggest that the release of this book, or any book for that matter, cannot help but coincide with some future Kevin Bacon project due to Mr. Bacon's fecundity. For convenience's sake, I offer to conduct the interview on the phone or in person, as I live just around the corner from Mr. Bacon in New York City and see him on the street or in the garage with his kids quite often and we smile at each other and pet each other's dogs. I will need an hour of Mr. Bacon's life, at most. For credibility, I list my agent, my editor, my publisher, my history, my height, weight, age, and the name of my dog, Lulu.

E-mails go back and forth, details and dates and such, until Molly reports that Mr. Bacon has agreed. Swell. Glitter. Now all I have to do is contact Mr. Bacon's lawyer, says Molly. I call Fred Gaines and leave a message. After a few days, I leave another message. And then another. In danger of becoming a nuisance, I contact Molly for assistance. Swell. Fred Gaines calls me.

"I have to tell you," he says, "I'm uncomfortable with the fact you told PMK that I didn't return your calls."

"But you didn't return any calls," I say.

"What do you want?" Fred Gaines wants to know.

"I'm calling you because PMK told me to call you."

"Why?" he asks.

"I have no idea," I say.

"I don't either," he says.

"What do we do now?" I ask.

"Send me all the pertinent information about the book and the questions you intend to ask Mr. Bacon and I will find out what's going on and get back to you."

I do. He doesn't. Time goes by. I hear from neither lawyer nor PMK. I write an e-mail.

"Dear Molly, Sorry to bother you again, but you seem to be the only competent person on the Kevin Bacon case. I finally spoke to

Fred Gaines, and he had no idea why anyone asked me to speak to him, or him to me. I just want to talk to Kevin Bacon. I think Osama bin Laden might be easier."

I get an instant e-mail from Joy Fehily. Who? Joy Fehily. VP at PMK.

"Bruce—Molly is my assistant and I see all her e-mails. To call Mr. Bacon's attorney and publicist incompetent reflects poorly on you. I will let Mr. Bacon know of your opinion."

I write back to Joy Fehily and tell her if I ever get a chance to talk to Mr. Bacon, I would be happy to deliver my opinions in person. These are, I am sad to report, the last unglittering words you will read about Mr. Bacon in this book, for the next and last e-mail I receive from Joy Fehily is curt:

"Bruce—Mr. Bacon's schedule is very busy at this time. Unfortunately, he is not available."

At Broad and Chestnut, a toothless man has his hand out.

"Can you help me?" he asks.

I put a dollar in his hand.

"I need two dollars," he says.

"Why?"

"Chicken wings cost two dollars," he says.

We discuss nutrition for a minute. I do most of the discussing. He is just hungry. His luck is down, his cost of living up. Why shouldn't panhandlers ask for a raise? Inflation takes its toll on everyone. Coat check girls still get a dollar. Valet parkers still get a dollar. I wonder if the bellhop in front of the Park Hyatt gets the same tips he did five years ago, ten years ago, maybe twenty.

"Can I ask you a few questions about gratuities?" I say.

"You need Tolstoy," says the bellhop.

"I prefer talking to someone who works here."

"Tolstoy," he insists. "He's the bellman. Around the corner."

Indeed. Joe Tolstoy stands sentry at the main door in Chancellor

Court. He is tall and upright and apparently a ranking member of the Hyatt Brigade, donning a white uniform with three gold stripes on the sleeve and a proper military hat. He is not gregarious. He is a bellman.

"Have tips gone up?" I ask.

"Bellhops make more money than bellmen, but I like my job better," he says, and then stands at relaxed attention. Bellhops need to be alert, ready to scurry about and take luggage from hither to yon; bellmen greet, open doors, smile, compliment the kids, hail a cab, offer advice.

"Have tips increased over the years?" I ask.

"Pulling up to such an elegant hotel puts pressure on people, and they usually do the right thing."

"Tolstoy, how much is the normal tip?"

"A dollar a bag is standard," Tolstoy finally 'fesses up.

"Thank you."

"A dollar per person for hailing a cab is also standard."

"How does it ever increase?" I ask.

"It hasn't changed in a long time, but no one is telling the world that bellmen need more money. To be honest, gratuities are not on my mind when doing my job. I've been around long enough to know that if you provide each guest with outstanding service, at the end of the shift, my day will have been worthwhile, both in terms of satisfaction and finance."

"You serious, Tolstoy?" I ask.

"I am," says Tolstoy.

"Can you say that again?" I ask.

"Even a slow day is rewarding when one is surrounded by the wonderful people that swirl around downtown Philadelphia on a daily basis."

"Are you pulling my leg, Tolstoy?"

"No. A fortunate man doesn't necessarily have to make a fortune."

Tolstoy is dipping into his lit bag now. He says he's only read the short stories of his namesake, but he carries on the tradition in his own way: Tolstoy is a screenwriter.

After Cardinal Dougherty High School, Tolstoy went to Temple. Since graduation, he has written four unsold screenplays. The last one is a variation on the Bertolucci film called "Last Tango in Philly." Cream cheese instead of butter? Another script is about a Philly boy who works at a ritzy hotel and moonlights as a screenwriter and gets involved with the mishugas of the guests.

Tolstoy will not let me read his screenplays. No matter how much I hector him, he stands pat. I give him a tip anyway. Here it is:

"Get out of Philadelphia, Tolstoy."

"Why?" he asks.

"If you are serious about screenwriting, get out. You're in the Philly Dance of Death. Cardinal Dougherty, Temple, Center City, Job for Life. You either get out when you're young and full of beans, or you spend the rest of your days wondering how the other half lives."

Tolstoy listens politely. I tell him he will meet a girl, fall in love, move to the burbs, get stuck with a mortgage, and that will be that. A gargantuan effort is required to escape this not-ready-for-prime-time city.

"Hollywood is a million miles away from the Park Hyatt," I say.

"M. Night Shyamalan did it," says Tolstoy.

"M. Night Shyamalan is a freak."

" 'Cause he talks to dead people?" asks Tolstoy.

"No. All Hindus do that. Shyamalan was the only devout little Hindu boy who grew up in South Philly and attended Episcopal Academy on the Main Line and signed a multimillion-dollar deal with Disney. He's afraid to fly, so he uses Philly as his back lot. He's a freak. One in a trillion."

"Really?"

"Really. You gotta fly, Joe, fly. Philly will squeeze the juice out of you and then stomp all over your seeds."

"Tell you the truth, this is not how I planned it."

"I know, Joe. Nothing works out the way you planned it."

"Mind if I give you a tip now?" asks Tolstoy.

"Not at all."

"Things are changing here," he says.

"Changing?"

"In the past couple years. Changing."

"How so, Joe?"

"If you're any good at what you do, you'll find out. Maybe some things do work out. Gotta get back to work now. Another nice family has just pulled up."

11

QUE NINGÚN NIÑO SE QUEDA ATRÁS

Sansom Street to Locust Street

A T the corner of Broad and Sansom is a newsstand. My grandfather worked at one of the many newsstands in Center City. He didn't sell newspapers or cigarettes. He sold hope, a sucker's bet. He wrote numbers. A newsstand was a good place to write numbers because lots of people passed by every day and money changed hands without suspicion and the winning numbers were right there in the paper, the last three digits of the race track's handle. That's the only part my grandfather could read, the numbers. His stated profession, for the purpose of family discussions and government welfare, was house painter.

I met him six or seven times, at holiday dinners, at my bar mitzvah. He smoked and coughed and wore baggy brown suits with yellowed pinstripes. He didn't have many teeth or much hair. I always wondered why he didn't shave for the occasions. You'd think he would have shaved for such occasions. He was quiet during the meals, no matter how festively argumentative they were.

My mother said he was a stupid man with nothing to say.

My Uncle Max would say it is better to keep quiet and let people think you are stupid than open your mouth and prove it.

My grandfather's name was Joseph Goldstein. He was an immigrant from Russia. He had three daughters and one son. During the Great Depression, he hit the road looking for work and trying to bring home some bacon. The family did not adhere to Jewish culinary laws. After a year or so, he was officially marked down as abandoning his family, a branding that was held against him until the day he died. When he did return to Philadelphia with no bacon, he sold apples on a street corner. He must have grown accustomed to street corners. From apples to numbers in one lifetime.

My cousin Bobb—that's right, three b's, he's an artist, worked with Warhol, invented multimedia, prefers three b's—recently told me that anytime he did poorly on a test in high school, his father would admonish him: "You want to grow up to be like Joe Goldstein? Get to work!"

Everything else I know about my grandfather I know from my mother. She hated him and blamed him for everything traumatic in her life except the death of my father. The responsibility for that capital crime was reserved for me.

That's all I know about my grandfather. I don't know what Russian shtetl he left or why he married my grandmother or why he left her. She died before I was born. I never asked my grandfather anything personal, so I don't know what he dreamed about before arriving in America or how he ended up running numbers in Philadelphia. When it comes to family matters, I am a coward. Maybe I inherited that gene from him. I don't investigate my lineage. I don't ask, they don't tell.

I call my brother.

"Which newsstand did Grandpop work at?" I ask.

"He worked at a newsstand?" he asks back.

"When he ran numbers," I say.

"He ran numbers?"

"Are you kidding?"

"No," says my brother. "I've never heard this before."

"What do you think your grandfather did?"

"He sold balloons on Broad Street," he says.

"He did?"

"At the Thanksgiving Day Parade and Mummers."

"That's two days a year."

"It left him a lot of time for the track," says my brother.

"He played the ponies?" I ask.

"I spent a day with him at Liberty Bell."

"He took you to the track?"

"I met him there, by accident. He knew everyone, so I figured that's what he did."

"How did he do at the track?" I ask.

"Don't ask."

"Did you learn anything about him?" I ask.

"Sure. He never bet quinellas."

"Do you remember hearing that he was a house painter?" I ask.

"That sounds familiar," says my brother. "Two coats, one day?"

"That was Mel Brooks describing Hitler."

"Oh. I knew someone from Germany was a house painter."

"Your grandfather was from Russia."

"He was?"

"Do you remember our other grandfather?" I ask.

"We had another grandfather?"

"Talk to you later," I say.

I met my father's father once on Long Island. He was a pleasant man, with his thick accent and his homemade vest. He seemed too short to have sired five six-foot-plus sons. I didn't mention this to him.

When my mother's father died, my brother and I were on either side of the casket, carrying him to the hearse in silence. My brother asked, "If your last name was Bearer, what's the last thing you would name your son?" I cracked up. My grandfather would have been dropped if not for the four men who found no humor in the comment. Funerals get less funny as you get older.

I have no ties to anyplace or anything other than Philadelphia. Without it, I'd have no roots at all. Like so many of my generation, I am Jewish by acculturation, devoid of training in the Talmud, and with no reason to believe in it. Or is it the Torah I'm supposed to believe? The world is besotted with religions born of equally flimsy and profound narratives. Zen Buddhism is the easiest to swallow and the hardest to practice. It's Zen.

I love and hate Philadelphia more than anyplace I know, which is the basis of a meaningful relationship, I suppose. I don't love it because I lived here. I love it because it lives in me.

At the corner of Broad and Walnut, a couple is looking up at the street sign, and then at each other, and then back at the street sign, and then back at each other. Bewildered, they look around the intersection until one turns to the other and asks, "What the hell happened to Fourteenth Street?"

"This is it," I interject. "This is Fourteenth Street."

"This is Broad Street," says the missus.

"Broad Street is Fourteenth Street," I say.

They remain bewildered.

"Starting at the Delaware River," I say, "the streets go from Front to thirteen and then comes Broad and then the numbers continue, fifteen through twenty-five."

"And then what?" she asks.

"You're in the Schuylkill River."

"That's it? That's midtown?" she asks.

"We call it Center City. Ten blocks by twenty-five. Cozy, huh?"

No sooner do the incredulous middle-aged middle-American tourists cross Fourteenth Street in the middle of the white lines than an Asian couple—don't ask what country, please—asks for directions to the Avenue of the Arts.

"This is the Avenue of the Arts," I say.

"This not Broad Street?" asks the Asian husband.

"Yes, it's Broad Street and Avenue of the Arts, at the same time, until it's just Broad Street again and not Avenue of the Arts anymore."

"Ah," he says.

"Are you looking for something special?" I ask.

"For Gamble and Huff studio. Sound of Philadelphia."

"It's two blocks that way," I say, pointing south. "Right across the street from the Academy of Music."

"Across from Academy of Music. Ah. Thank you."

That juxtaposition sums up the scene: the Sound of Philadelphia across from the Academy of Music; Gamble, Huff, and Bell staring down Stokowski, Ormandy, and Muti; the hits of the 1970s wafting across the street and the century to the first opera hall in America, opened circa 1857.

Gamble and Huff wrote or produced 170 gold or platinum soul records with smoky horns, percussive strings, pulsating bass lines, and a pre-disco beat or superslow grind ballads. You know their songs.

How important are they to the precise and eclectic musical tastes of the Philadelphia citizenry? We shall let the staff of *Philadelphia Weekly*, the hip downtown free paper, circulation of 100,000, answer that question. In a recent poll of the top 100 Philly songs of all time—and how many of these would appear on any other city's list?—Gamble and Huff took win, place, and show, and throw in number nine too. (LaBelle strayed from Philly only now and then, but recorded "Lady Marmalade" in New Orleans.)

1.   "Expressway to Your Heart," Soul Survivors
2.   "Love Train," The O'Jays
3.   "Me and Mrs. Jones," Billy Paul
4.   "Rock Around the Clock," Bill Haley & the Comets
5.   "The Fever," Bruce Springsteen Bootleg
6.   "Rich Girl," Hall & Oates
7.   "Hello It's Me," Todd Rundgren

8.   "All You Zombies," Hooters
9.   "I Don't Love You Anymore," Teddy Pendergrass
10.   "Lady Marmalade," LaBelle

As the Asian couple walks away, I wonder what songs they danced to when they were young. "TSOP" by MFSB? Maybe they performed karaoke on their honeymoon to "Ain't No Stoppin' Us Now" or "The Love I Lost" by Harold Melvin & the Blue Notes. I'd love to sit down with them and talk music. I bet they know this is where Coltrane loved supreme, where Philly Joe jonesed, where Chubby Checker twisted, where the Delfonics la-la-la'd, where Hall felt his Oates, where Todd Rundgren still says "Hello It's Me," where Bruce became the Boss, where the Roots took hold, where Pink started her party, and where G. Love and Special Sauce serenade the same congested freeway, I-76, made famous in "Expressway to Your Heart" almost forty years before.

I could use a drink. Bliss, at Broad and Locust, was chosen by *Esquire* magazine as one of the best new restaurants in America. Bliss is a helluva lot to promise a thirsty wayfarer. The walls are backlit seascapes, reminding you of Aunt Cora's slide show of her Caribbean vacation. The blond bartender is cordial, the habitués pleasant, the vodka cold, but the star of the show is the Crispin Glover look-alike reciting the night's specials to a table of four. His performance rivals any ham in the nearby theaters, the Merriam, the Wilma, the Kimmel Center, or the Academy of Music. Appetizers by Molière, entrées by Ionesco, desserts pure Woody Allen. His audience quartet loves it. You fear the backlit seascapes may disappear, frond by freaking frond, as he chews up the scenery.

In a stage whisper, he recommends the Pekin duck breast with sweet potato purée and port wine reduction; he himself has had it seven times and loved it six; the one disappointing time, he explains dolefully, was due to a personal crisis, not involving the chef and certainly not the duck.

When not waiting on tables, John Sterling, like so many Philly twenty-somethings, is in a band, the guitarist for the countrified Sun-downers. He studied acting at Rutgers and dreamed of the silver screen until he followed his girlfriend to Cleveland, got dumped, and, naturally, fled to Las Vegas, where he ended up waiting tables at the MGM Grand. It was the closest he ever got to a movie career. Best-laid plans.

"I use my thespian training every night," he says. "If a table wants a show, I give them a show. Restaurants are showbiz."

"How does this compare to Vegas?" I ask.

"In Vegas, everyone arrived drunk for dinner," he says.

"Winners and losers?"

"Everyone. No one cared about the food."

"How was the food?"

"Decent. That's all I need. If the food is decent, I can make money."

"Why did you leave Vegas?"

"Two planes crashed into the Twin Towers," he says. "And I moved back home right away. To Audubon, New Jersey, to be near the people I loved, to be with my family."

"You're still there?"

"In Audubon, yes, but I'd rather work at the worst joint in Philly than the best joint in Jersey."

"I see," I say.

"Not that this, I mean Bliss, is the worst . . . you know what I mean. Fix it up for me. Gotta run. Showtime."

As Sterling returns to his table for act two, who should roll into Bliss but the Geator with the Heater, the Boss with the Hot Sauce, the Discophonic Dandy, the Man with a Thousand Names—Jerry Blavat. The disc jockey who rode hipness to the Triple Crown. He smiles at me as if we're old friends and I say, instinctively, vodka-lubricatedly, "Greetings and salutations—my man, pots 'n' pans." It was his signature hello on some small radio station in the early 1960s, when he played oldies before most people knew they were newies, where he had enough patter to talk over the platter and no one minded.

He played sweet soul music, obscure B sides by the Marvellos or Candy and the Kisses, as well as Lloyd Price and Fats Domino. He was the grooviest white man on the waves, and one of the youngest. Georgie Woods, the Man with the Goods, owned black radio, but here was this kid from South Philly—Italian or Jewish or Polish, who knew, who cared?—with a high-pitched voice, Negro intonation, hipster lingo, and a personal relationship with every singer he touted. He knew how serious the music was, how long it would live, not just bubblegum to be chewed and stuck under the desk. The gig was not for the money: he had to do this or die.

And here he is. The Geator with the Heater. Blissed out in Bliss. I thought he'd be the Geezer with the Wheezer by now, but he looks great, dances a spiffy little jig like a Sicilian leprechaun and tells you he works out every day and weighs the same 130 pounds he did when he danced on *American Bandstand* and went to Texas with his mentor, the ousted Bob Horn, the original host of *Bandstand* and the first grown-up we knew who was charged with sexually molesting the same Catholic school girls we all wanted to molest. Bob Horn was thirty-seven.

The Geator will spin his bio to anyone who wants to hear, dropping names like confetti on V-E Day as he recounts his days as a roadie, a television host, a radio personality, a record store owner, a music producer, a dance magnate, a sockhop tycoon, and a self-made dynamo who has yet to slow down. He is still on radio, television, at the Kimmel Center, at the Sands in Atlantic City, at Memories in Margate, on PBS doo-wop specials. He is on right now. He is so on that you'd hate to be around when he goes off, when he hits the dark side of the moon.

Someone at the bar has done Jerry Blavat "a solid" and Blavat wants to repay the do-gooder with a bottle of wine.

"Anything he wants," says the Geator, and snaps his fingers so loudly that people turn to see who uncorked the champagne. The Geator, digging the attention, snaps the fingers of his other hand just as loudly. The Geator's a switch-hittin' finger-snappin' sonuvagun.

Before we were exposed to Lenny Bruce, before we heard Lord Buckley, we had the Geator. He was Kerouac without the Columbia degree or cosmic vision; he had a stack of 45s instead of a roll of tele-type paper. He wasn't on the road, he was the road, the road to the other side of the tracks. He was the antidote to Dick Clark, that sani-tized salesman who knew so little about the music and cared less about teenagers.

Listen to Blavat promote his television show on his radio show in the summer of '65:

"Once again, it's the Big Boss with the Hot Sauce, the Teenage Leader, the Geator with the Heater, and the time has come, my lord, my liege, my champ! We wail out of sight and we don't wait for night. We play our tune in the afternoon. We put a scene on the screen that is naturally mean. We crack the whip and make everybody flip. And I'm gonna tell you why. Yeah, baby, listen to the Geator with the Heater. I'm gonna tell you why.

"You see, we've put on some variety that stones society. You know how? Well, we get wailers like the Four Tops, Len Barry and Mitch Ryder; drop in some daughters like Dee Dee Sharp and the Three De-grees; work some soul with Aretha Franklin; try a little jazz with Ramsey Lewis; knock on some drums with Olatunji; get the bad, bad voice of Arthur Prysock; and burn with the band of Fats Domino. That's a show.

"That's a show, baby, and that's what we do. We wail for you. It may be silly, but it's only in Philly; no sad song, it won't be long until we take our bow from Maine to Cal. And you too can do the Boogaloo. What's the Boogaloo? Well, you might ask me what the Philly Dog is or the Rain Dance or the national talk, the Discophonic Walk! They're dances, babe-ophonic baby, and they're all created by yon teenagers. No choreography, nobody's idea of what they think teenagers might dance like—this is it! A soulful group of Philly kids, not handpicked, just grabbed off the streets where the dances originate!"

Blavat's influence is still blaring in Philly. He is why the Philly sound is color-blind. Why a hospital ER will have "Hello It's Me" on the intercom. Why the diner plays "I Need Your Lovin'" by Don Gardner and Dee Dee Ford. Why Teddy P. still makes the girls swoon. Who's Teddy P? If you don't know him by now . . .

From the kitchen comes a guy who says a few words to the bartender, gets a drink, and then returns to the kitchen. He looks Mexican. I ask the bartender if the man speaks English. She wants to know why. I wonder if he's from San Mateo. She freezes. Patrons at the bar stop talking and start looking at me. One innocent question has altered the state of the bar. They want to know for whom I work, what agency of the government sent me, why I am snooping around. No, no, no, I say, you have it all wrong, I'm just curious. Illegals are a touchy topic. The workers may be put into jeopardy, the restaurant may get busted, and one of the owners of Bliss, Roseanne Martin, is "dating" Ed Snider, owner of the Flyers, the 76ers, and the arena in which they play. This is one small village.

No one knows how to deal with the Mexican in the middle of the room, or the kitchen, or the city, or the country.

These new settlers are unsettling: if they want to take our money and run, they have no need to conquer our language or embrace our ways and means; if they decide to stay, fall into good fortune or fall in love or fall for *la ciudad del amor brotherly,* they are going to take over, become the majority minority and then the first minority majority. Either way, folks are frightened.

No one mentions how improved our soccer teams will be.

Or points out that our beloved Billy Penn was never a citizen, never spent more than a couple years in the city he stands above. He sold real estate in London. Not very well. He died penniless.

It makes sense that Mexicans gravitate to South Philly. It's close to the foodie world of Center City, it's inexpensive, and it's Catholic. Mexicans might enjoy the saved resurrected Jesus of America after all those years of the bleeding suffering Jesus on Mexican crosses.

South Philly is parochial in another sense as well. It's where local luminaries like Joey Vento, owner of Geno's Steaks, can hang a sign that reads: "This is AMERICA. WHEN ORDERING, 'SPEAK EN-GLISH.'" That's what the national news covered. What the cameras missed was the next guy in line, the South Phillyffyan who ordered in English: "Yo cuz, gimme da steak ta go wid a boddla whodder." Señor Vento ought to realize that the culture of Philadelphia is so robust, so rooted, that his Italian/Mexican/Chinese great-grandchildren will be smashing piñatas with miniature Phillies bats and then enjoying queso jalapeño steak sandwiches with Spanish onions and shiitake mushrooms.

All the emigrants from Elsewhere, from the Yucatan and from Wyoming, from Cambodia and from Tennessee, may chip away at the hard-earned, honorable dyspepsia of Philadelphia, but they are not large enough in either number or spirit to smooth the hard edges of the city's fine disfigurement.

Fret not, Señor Vento.

12

A Child's School of Rock

Washington Avenue to Federal Street

A T Broad and Washington, the Marine Club, built in 1904, fills a square city block and once served as the Marine Quartermaster's Depot. Tens of thousands of U.S. soldiers were outfitted and equipped here during World War I; produced here were mosquito nets, mess pans, helmets, uniforms, foot lockers, and stoves. During World War II, uniforms, tents, lockers, and bunks were manufactured here twenty-four hours a day. Now, in the time of condos, being on the southernmost border of Avenue of the Arts, close to Center City yet removed from the congestion, Marine Club has been converted by EB Realty into two hundred apartments for yuppies and students.

"You a Marine?" I hear someone ask as I look through the war artifacts in the first-floor hallway.

"No. You?" I ask.

"No. I'm just the super. Marines used to live here. Before they shipped out. Some guys stop by every so often for a visit."

"Not me," I say.

Two pubescent girls prance through the lobby, down the steps, and out the door. They speak in a foreign tongue and wear a ton of makeup.

"Rock School," says the super.

"Rock School?"

"Across the street," he says. "The Rock School. Those girls. They're students there."

"And they live here?"

"We have a whole floor from the Rock School. They come from all over the world. Those two, they say they come from Georgia."

"You don't believe them?"

"Did you hear them? Sounds like they're talking Russian."

"They looked like Britney and Christina," I say.

"I don't know why they wear so much makeup. They just sweat it off. You know that MTV show, *The Real World*? That's what it's like around here. You hear lots of stories in my position."

"You feel like sharing some stories?" I ask.

"I don't deal in gossip. I'm a Buddhist."

"Oh," I say. "Did you see the documentary?"

"What documentary?"

"*Rock School*," I say.

"With Jack Black?"

"No, Paul Green."

"Can't say I have," he says.

I have. It was very cool, a three-act rock 'n' roll version of *The Bad News Bears*, with Paul Green as charismatic as Walter Matthau and just as foul-mouthed and beloved, only it was nonfiction. Green's teaching technique involves using the F word more than the C chord. He threatens students with the retelling of the story of how he lost his virginity. Green is a silver-tongued egomaniac who teaches with such persuasion and intimidation that it works; if he taught pacifism, the city would be lousy with pimply-faced Gandhis. These misfits, flunkies, desperadoes, Amish freaks, and Cobain wannabes find a musical oasis, kindred spirits, a father figure, and one supremely simple lesson: practice makes you better. They start out awed by a Frank Zappa chart and end up mastering it. The experience prepares them for almost anything. Conquering a Mozart sonata or an Eddie Van Halen solo will bring a smile to your soul and security to your inner adult. Paul Green thinks it makes you a better person.

"The humanities are philosophy, literature, poetry, music. That's what makes us human. To hone our craft is to hone our humanity, and that's what I want the kids to do. There is true happiness that comes with confidence."

I can't wait to see this Paul Green in action.

I cross Broad Street, still 114 feet wide, and enter the Rock School.

In the cushy lobby are decorous parents holding small hypoallergenic dogs or large mocha latte decafs. They don't look like parents worried about or freely endorsing a drug-addled, sex-saturated life for their rock star darling offspring. Told the fourth floor is where the action is, I take the elevator. The doors open onto a large room with skylights, mirrors, barres, an older woman playing Chopin on a piano, and two dozen young females limbering up as if for a Capezio commercial directed by Edgar Degas. Black leg warmers over pink stockings, pink leg warmers over black stockings with seams, pink skirts, black shorts, shorter shorts, unitards with long sleeves and short sleeves and no sleeves at all; body tights and leotards, and one leopard skin leotard. They are all wearing makeup. The two girls from the Marine Club lobby are here. They are speaking Russian.

Wait a minute. The music is definitely not Zappa and the students are definitely not ax-toting outsiders in Goth costumes. These are serious little dancers. Light, sweet, crude. The teacher bangs his hands in a thunderclap and the girls (and six boys) go through a series of glissades and fouettes until another thunderclap halts them. The clapper is not Paul Green. He is Chris Fleming. He takes a deep breath, his potbelly expands, and he says, much to his own delight, "Terrible. Just terrible."

Something is terribly wrong. I am standing here, pen in hand, mouth agape, wondering how I walked into a rock 'n' roll school and found budding ballerinas and danseurs. What happened to the infamous Paul Green and his School of Rock?

I take the elevator back to where it came from. Turns out I have stumbled into an internationally acclaimed ballet factory named for its benefactor, Milton Rock. This is the Rock School all right. But not *that* rock school. My head is pirouetting. Let's back up. Paul Green started his School of Rock in Philly in 1998. Milton Rock bailed out the troubled Pennsylvania Ballet by purchasing this building and re-naming it the Rock School in 2000. Jack Black starred in the fictional movie *School of Rock* in 2003, written by Mike White and bearing a marked similarity to Paul Green's actual life. And *Rock School*, the documentary about Paul Green, debuted in 2005.

What's black and white and green all over? The School of Rock.

The Rock School houses six dance studios and serves four hundred students. Ego and philanthropy do not always make graceful dance partners. Uncle Miltie could have chosen a less confusing name.

Undaunted by this rock turmoil, I return to the fourth floor straightaway.

As the woman plays the piano, the faunlets show off their discipline, their willingness, their acrobatic prowess, their sweaty little asses. High culture crashes on the rocks of low culture and washes me ashore, somewhere between rectitude and lust. What would Buddha do? WWBD? After another complicated step is taught, with axials and leaps, the best students in the school, which means some of the best students in the world, show off their talent. "Are you all drunk?" the teacher yells. Chris Fleming, by all accounts, is an excellent teacher and choreographer, having earned his tights at the NYC Ballet, but he seems perpetually annoyed about something. He is also hands-on. In these days of touchy parents and miscreant adults, it is risky to be known as a hands-on teacher, but there is no way around it. Chris Fleming touches every student, pushing, pulling, twisting, turning, yanking, nudging, bumping. At one point, disgusted, needing a moment, needing drama, he leaves the class in limbo and walks to the large picture window and stares through it.

What he sees on the northeast corner of Broad and Washington, if he is looking, is a lot of nothing. A huge and valuable lot of nothing at the entrance of the Avenue of the Americas owned by Holt Logistics Management. Six acres in search of a business. Leo Holt likes to say, "I just sit back and watch the values rise." Mr. Holt has been pushed, pulled, twisted, turned, yanked, nudged, and bumped by greengrocers, residential developers, commercial savants, ethnic entrepreneurs, and suave mountebanks. He's sitting back and watching the value rise. There was a movie studio and recording facility blueprinted for the spot by Will Smith and his brother Harry, but that fell through. Once a year, the Cirque du Soleil appears on the empty lot. That's it. One week a year, lots of adult bodies in pink and black spandex fly around the empty space.

"The city deserves the right enterprise in that spot," says Leo Holt. "I am in no hurry. I just sit back and watch the values explode."

Some people in the area wish the four *Beacons* would explode too. They are forty-two-foot-high metal and glass pylons on each corner of Broad and Washington. They resemble very tall and very rigid cotton candy, twinkling in the sun and lit from within at night. The colors of the glass change with the distance and angle of the viewer. They are not easy to like. The person who dislikes them most is the artist who created them.

"My experience was so nasty, so hideous, I can't look at those pieces. I lost all taste for that area." Ray King worked on the *Beacons* in 1994. And '95. And '96. And hopes never to see them again.

After he won a contest, beating out 475 other artists, King got down to work. A city engineer got to work too, planting the concrete footings for the eventual *Beacons* forty feet deep. On all four corners. In all the wrong places. Ramps for the disabled would run smack into the sculptures, and wheelchairs would be sent reeling back into the street from whence they came. King feared lawsuits and ugliness would surely ensue. Lawsuits and ugliness ensued. While different factions did legal battle, there was dirt on the four corners. For five years. Piles of dirt and stumps. Disabled art.

"I lost $50,000 of my own," says Ray King. "It almost sent me into bankruptcy. I chased the city around for the last payment before I would install it. It choked my studio for four years. It was the most heinous experience of my artistic life. Right now, I am working on projects in England, Italy, Taiwan, California, and Florida, so I have nothing against public art or municipal funding—only Philadelphia."

Finally, just in time for the millennium, with the help of then mayor Ed Rendell, the *Beacons* went up. The reviews were mixed. They are not things you fall in love with right off the bat. Or maybe ever. At night, they sparkle. They make the corner safe. The homeless sleep on the smooth black surfaces of their bases.

I hear a deep male voice say, "Welcome to Route C." I look around. I see nothing but a city bus at a red light. It's a talking bus. Sounding more like Hal in *2001* than a South Philly wiseguy, the bus talks and blinks and roots for the home team. In the destination box, above the windshield, it flashes GO EAGLES! GO EAGLES!

The mural at Wharton Street makes Frank Sinatra look like an anorexic Oscar Levant. Four stories high (which Frank occasionally was), surrounded by fans (which Frank usually was), Sinatra croons to fans of all colors; one couple near the second floor is fainting.

The little secret of the Murals Project is that people and businesses can sponsor this art, put up the ideas and the money. Sinatra was paid for by Jack Daniel's (Frank's favorite beverage), Jerry Blavat, Comcast, the *Daily News,* and Frederick's (not of Hollywood, but) of local restaurant fame. With all that muscle, they should have a better mural.

Sinatra and his *Ocean's 11* gang could not knock over the Mobil station beneath the mural. Everything except the petrol is behind bulletproof plastic. You ask the attendant through a bankteller's slit if you can use the lavatory and he shakes his head no. Why not? The door is locked and no one is allowed in or out. The last time I pulled into a station on Broad Street, in a VW Bug, someone pumped the gas, checked the oil, cleaned the windshield, and handed over the key to the men's room. Now you do your own pumping and damn your bladder. A block south of Sinatra is Mario Lanza on a four-story wall with four stories: tuxedoed Mario as Caruso, darkened Mario as Othello, saddened Mario as Pagliacci, humble Mario as hometown boy cum international bon vivant. On a low wall seventy feet wide are the names of people who contributed $500 or more to the mural. Lots of names. South Philly boys who make it big are never forgotten.

Directly across the street is a car wash for $2.95.

Starting somewhere around Tasker or Morris, cars are parked, with impunity, down the middle of the street, on the median, facing north and south, wherever a concrete island does not prevent such a thing. For some reason, this is legal in South Philly, or at least not illegal. Residents thank dear departed Frank Rizzo for implementing the laissez-faire attitude; yo, we needed more parking space, so it's only common sense. Two lanes still move north and south, while cars are parked on both sides of Broad Street and down the middle. The firemen at Firehouse Engine #1, Ladder #5, say they have no problem with the practice, even when they have to respond to an emergency during rush hour. Car after car, block after block, without a single citation on a windshield. This does not happen on North Broad Street.

South Philly has its own rules. Ask someone raised near 5th and Shunk where he was raised and he will say 5th and Shunk. He will not say Phillyffya. Or even South Phillyffya. South Phillyffyans tend to reduce the world to a corner. And then park as near as possible.

The gold-stenciled lettering on the window near Morris Street says ROCCO TARELLE'S TAILORS, but there's only Rocco. He charges $550 to construct a suit nowadays and turns out five a week. Used to do fifteen, then down to ten and now half that many. Sure, he could make more suits if he had the energy or the desire; sure, he could buy the material and do the fitting and cutting and mail the parts to Costa

Rica and they would send back the finished suit, ready to wear, cost-effective, and sure he'd be competitive. Rocco sneers at the strategy. He gets tired just thinking about it.

"Outsourcing has changed the name of the game," he says. "The Gap, Men's Wearhouse, Jos. A. Bank—they outsource everything. Asia, Latin America, anywhere they can. Who can compete with foreign labor? Who wants to? I give the parts to my old friends who work at home. We're a dying breed and we stick together. Loyalty is a dying breed. They do the stitching and lining. I pay them decent money. Once I am gone, there will be no more tailors like me. Maybe the Mexicans will take over the shop, if anybody still wants a handmade suit."

Rocco, sixty-eight, pallid and mild-mannered, refuses to hire another tailor. There has been change enough in his three decades at this address. His wife passed, and too many friends. Broad Street itself seems like a foreign place to him. So Rocco clings to one unaltered thing: himself.

"Alterations?" he sneers. "You can make a living doing alterations. Know why? You charge someone $20 an hour and you keep the whole $20 an hour. No responsibility, no investment in material, no nothing. But who cares about alterations? I am a tailor. I create from whole cloth."

Rocco has four sons.

"Two are lawyers, one a doctor, and one a businessman. They wear suits, they don't make them. Let me tell you something about sons. If you make them independent, you won't see them very often. If you keep them dependent, they won't be happy. Neither will you. Some choices in this life, huh? I tell them, 'Don't wait for me to ask for anything—I will never ask.' I refuse to be a burden. That would shame me and put them in a terrible spot. But if they should ask me for something, that would make me happy, and them too. Ask me. Please. Ask me for something."

One father left behind.

The phone rings. The call is from Italy. The upstairs tenant, who spends half the year in the Old Country, in Sicily, is returning soon and he needs something taken care of in his apartment. Rocco excuses himself and speaks Italian into the phone.

Thin streams of sunlight illuminate the dust particles in the dark tailor shop. I miss my sons. As Rocco talks into the phone, he picks some lint from a newly made single-breasted suit, brown with wide white pinstripes and wide lapels, a garment from another era. You could see a young Frank Sinatra in this suit, crooning in front of the Tommy Dorsey band, eyes closed, bobby-soxers all atwitter. Suddenly, the brown suit, and then other suits, all the suits in the shop, are mere shells, missing their inhabitants, and Rocco is surrounded by well-dressed ghosts in this chiaroscuro.

"*Nessun problema, ciao, ciao,*" says Rocco and hangs up the phone.

"I write poetry," he says to me. "I'm not saying I'm Robert Frost, but I jot down some thoughts. Here. I have this notebook . . ."

He reaches under the counter and produces a black and white composition notebook. You expect to see a cigar box next, filled with Ticonderoga No. 2 yellow pencils, a pair of rounded safety scissors, and Elmer's Glue. Rocco hands me his notebook of poems. He is modest about his musings, and has every right to be. I read this one out loud:

i found this place when i was ten
it's where i met life's best friend
never knowing my length of stay
was it work or was it play
the treasures that abound within
renewed each day born again
a lure which builds upon itself
enriching one to living wealth
the place I learned to earn my keep
where I was taught to laugh and weep . . .
wafting winds upon the sand

will not erase imprinted hands
he stayed too long! some may think
but I sure would love another drink
time spent here is not measured on clocks
this oasis dear friends is my sandbox

"I've been a tailor for fifty-seven years," says Rocco. "And I often wonder how my life would have turned out if I had gone to the school after my father died. I was very young, and my mother wanted me to go to this overnight school, but my older brother wanted me around, to help with his business, so he taught me the tailor's trade. Otherwise, I would have gone to this school in North Philadelphia. I'm not complaining, but I often wonder how my life would have been different if I went to that school. It's called Girard College. Ever hear of it?"

"Yes, I've heard of Girard College," I say, and say no more. I am stunned by the largeness of the coincidence, the smallness of the city, the connectedness of us all; I say no more out of respect for his fantasy.

What I don't say to this decent man in his shop of empty suits is that not going to Girard College may have been the luckiest break he ever caught. The aftershocks of my relocation still register every time I open my mouth; a stutter began the day I was extirpated from my mother, my brother, my home, my school, my chums, my neighborhood, my street games, my girlfriends, my frozen foods, my security, my aunts, my uncles, my cousins, my equilibrium, my front porch, my awning, my glider, my corner grocer, my corner candy store, my moorings, my part of Broad Street. None of this do I mention to the tailor.

I call my brother. I get his voicemail. He did not go to Girard College. Whenever my mother would talk about it, in my years at Girard before my brother was old enough to enter, I told her to spare him the regimen, the rigors, and other activities left unspecified by me and uninvestigated by her. As much as I'd like to say I had a hand in my brother not attending Girard, it's not true.

The school rejected him. Girard College proved wiser, or more timid, than his own mother. He would not have done well with mandatory athletics and classrooms a half mile from the dorms, not with his heart murmur, his enlarged valve, and his frightening asthma attacks that required emergency room visits. Girard was a hard place. A thousand fatherless boys—some with no family at all—were in no mood to ooze compassion to the halt or lame, to any spaz or oddball who showed up with a doctor's note entitling him to skip gym or circumvent kitchen duty or beg off goddamn battalion practice on a cold winter's day. Boys with dead fathers were generally pissed off about their own raw deals, and that volatile admixture of grief and hostility was not diluted, more likely strengthened, by the fact that the single subject that was never discussed, not privately, not publicly, not in large groups or small, was the only common element that had redefined their lives, and had landed them, us, together in this walled place: dead fathers.

No one ever mentioned it.

Girard did not want my little brother. And I didn't want him at Girard. And his mother didn't want him home. And he knew it, knew it all, and he still stings from the knowing.

I leave him a nice message on his voicemail and look for someplace to eat. The Oriental Chinese Restaurant at Broad and Moore is a plain rectangular room filled with Asians. This is a good sign. With a $10 order, you get a free egg roll. Another good sign. I order vegetable brown rice. The waiter laughs, thinks I am kidding. This is a bad sign. No brown rice. I request General Tso's chicken. I hope he doesn't miss it, I say. The waiter doesn't laugh. I don't get a free egg roll.

Eight o'clock sharp is when services begin at the Abundant Life Chinese Mennonite Church. Services are offered in Cantonese, Mandarin, Indonesian, and sometimes English. No English tonight. One long room is decorated as plainly as the Chinese restaurant across the street, with an office in the rear instead of a kitchen. There are fifty comfortable red chairs ($1,680). Almost matching vermilion drapes

($685) cover the windows. Walls are white. Pastor Troung Tu delivers a sermon in Chinese and then turns on the electronic equipment ($1,290) and everyone sings along: eight Asian women, one African-American man, two little boys running amok and launching paper airplanes. The boys sing extemporaneously as they play, Chinese scat. Loudly. Joyfully. No one pays them much mind, even when they become fascinated with the Occidental stranger sitting in the rear of the room. They sit in front of the stranger, facing him on their knees, and stare into his blue eyes. Then they move next to him. And touch his white mustache. And then one boy, the three-year-old with a bunny rabbit T-shirt, sits on the lap of the Occidental stranger and starts to hit him with a Chinese hymnal. The stranger quietly repairs to the office to minimize the distraction. The kids follow unstealthily. On the floor of the office is a metal drain, suggesting this might have been, in fact, a restaurant kitchen at some point. One of the kids pretends he is peeing into the drain, and finds this hilarious. His younger friend mimics the pantomime. The Occidental stranger watches the two young boys pretending to pee and he misses his own sons.

The service is over. Women retrieve the little boys.

The money spent on every item in the church is part of the annual report that sits on the office desk, available to everyone.

Prayer time begins. The women form three groups. After some silence, one in each group starts to pray out loud, asking for heavenly guidance and forgiveness. Ten, fifteen minutes. Sometimes in Chinese, sometimes in English. Chinglish? Then it's around the horn. Each woman in each cluster speaks fervently, personally, overlappingly like a Robert Altman movie, like Mennonites at their first meetings in Philadelphia 320 years ago.

"Mennonite? We not Mennonite," says Grace Dith when prayers end. "They help us with money, so we say we Mennonite. We not Mennonite. Mennonite don't like jewelry or modern world. We not Mennonite."

These are, however, very conservative Christians. Grace's father was a minister in the Old Country and soon he will lead a march on Washington, D.C., to rally for traditional marriages between men and women.

"Where are the men tonight?" I ask.

"Men where men should be," says Grace.

"And where's that?"

"Working."

Her friends giggle.

"One out of five people in world Chinese," says Grace. "We over a billion people. We don't stay in Chinatown no more. We move to South Philly when housing affordable. North Philly too. We coming more and more. We move anywhere we want now."

Her friends giggle again. Almost 4 percent of the city's population is Asian, or seventy thousand, according to the last census. Most of the newly arrived have landed in Olney or South Philly, having come from Vietnam, Cambodia, and Laos—countries we napalmed during the Nixon years, openly and secretly.

After the two little boys strafe me with paper planes, I walk into the South Philly night thinking about Chinese women whose families migrated to Vietnam to escape the Japanese brutality during World War II who now pray to Jesus Christ on comfortable red chairs in a plain room on an ordinary weekday night on Broad Street in Philadelphia. The sky is small and low. The stars are dim. The statue of Billy Penn, the First Immigrant, shines inordinately brightly tonight.

At Broad and McKean, I stop at St. Ag's to take a leak. The hospital is now billed as the Thomas Jefferson Methodist Mercy St. Agnes Medical Center for Acute or Continuing Care. Health care businesses are merging faster than funeral homes or banks, and much more ecumenically. I cannot find the bathrooms on the first floor. I ask at the front desk. I must appear incapable of following my own nose, for a woman escorts me. She is a very nice woman. The lavatory is a very nice lavatory. After splashing some water on my face, I inquire about renting a room for the night. No one at the front desk takes me seriously.

"Do you know what they charge for a room in Center City?" I ask.

"Not really," says the nice woman.

"The Ritz has a room for $1,500," I say.

"That's more than we charge," she says.

"Exactly. And the $1,500 doesn't include a sponge bath or a morphine drip. And room service is extra. And parking is extra. And you have to tip too. Do you know how much to tip these days?"

"Can't say as I do," she says.

"Anyone ever give you a tip?" I ask.

"We do not accept gratuities."

"You see—I saved money already," I say. "Do you have room in your skilled nursing facility?"

"Do you need skilled nursing care?" she asks.

"Isn't it obvious?"

"You have to be referred by a doctor," she says.

"I can do that," I say. "My doctor's name is—"

"You're talking to the wrong person," she says. "Here, call this number in the morning."

She hands me a business card and a brochure all about the Thomas Jefferson Methodist Mercy St. Agnes Medical Center for Acute or Continuing Care. It's a mouthful all right. And a strange mongrel of a conglomeration, pairing a fourth-century teenage virgin martyr who is not recognized by Methodists and a nineteenth-century Deist president who had an affair with his African-American teenage slave, the half-sister of his wife. None of this is of interest to the nice lady at the front desk. She has work to do.

St. Agnes was a beautiful upper-crust Italian virgin who promised Jesus she would be married only to him. Why she would say this is anybody's guess. Despite this, or because of this, according to *Catholic Forum,* Agnes was taken to a Roman temple by several young men who tortured her when she refused to turn away from God. Some men offered her marriage. Agnes, thirteen years old, made the sign of the cross and opted to accept death before sacrificing her virginity. That's how one version of the story goes. Another one has Agnes refusing to marry a prefect's son, so she was sentenced to death, but Roman law forbade the murder of virgins, so the prefect ordered her raped so he could kill her. When the bundle of wood at her feet would not burn, miraculously according to some, the officer in charge cut off her head.

The actual forensic cause of death is fuzzy. *Catholic Forum* puts it this way: "beheaded and burned, or tortured and stabbed to death, or stabbed in the throat (sources vary) on 21 January 304 (sources vary) at Rome." Any way you slice it, it's brutal. It makes you reconsider how tough North Philly really is.

St. Agnes is now the patron saint of chastity, crops, gardeners, Girl Scouts, virgins, rape victims, engaged couples, and the diocese of Rockville Centre, New York. Don't ask.

What Agnes was not was a Methodist. Nor was Thomas Jefferson for that matter. Jefferson was many things—architect, archaeologist, astronomer, oenophile, philosopher, farmer, father, statesman, president, husband, father—but not a believer in the divinity of Jesus. He was raised an Anglican and practiced Unitarianism and called himself a Deist.

Deists believe in God but not supernatural revelation, not miracles, and not in the Bible, or any book, as the revealed word of any God. Jefferson possessed a serene conviction that Jesus' moral teachings were entirely compatible with natural law as it may be inferred from the sciences; a Unitarian view of Jesus.

In the newspapers and from the pulpits, he was accused of being an atheist and a Deist. While Evangelicals tried very hard to make Jefferson's religion a factor in the elections, his steadfast policy was to never respond to any attacks or make public statements concerning his faith. Privately, to John Adams, he wrote: "The whole history of these books [the Gospels] is so defective and doubtful that it seems vain to attempt minute enquiry into it: and such tricks have been played with their text, and with the texts of other books relating to them, that we have a right, from that cause, to entertain much doubt what parts of them are genuine. In the New Testament there is internal evidence that parts of it have proceeded from an extraordinary man; and that other parts are of the fabric of very inferior minds. It is as easy to separate those parts, as to pick out diamonds from dunghills."

It is no oversight that the Constitution has no mention of God. It prohibits any law banning religion, but relies on the nature of things, not the Holy Word. When Jefferson and other Deists mention God, they do not mean Jesus, or the father of Jesus. They mean Jehovah and Allah and the Creator who endowed all citizens with certain unalienable rights.

Seventeen seventy-six. The Age of Enlightenment.

It is getting late. My shoes need a rest from my feet. Time to find lodgings. This should be a snap. It is Tuesday. No particular Tuesday of no particular week. Just Tuesday. I walk back to Center City. Doubletree is sold out. Must be a convention. No, they say, tourists. Hyatt is sold out. Tourists. Radisson, sold out. Tourists. This is getting spooky. The Ritz-Carlton has one small room for $400. Are you kidding me? Who are all these people sleeping in my bed? Tourists.

Tourists in Philadelphia?

At the turn of the twentieth century, Philadullphia was not at the top of many destination lists. It was a defunct town of too many blue laws and blue-blooded attorneys, of broken bells and rampant crime. Nightlife was an oxymoron. The restaurant renaissance was confidential; you couldn't find it in *Zagat's* or a tragic Pete Dexter novel or a humorous Joe Queenan essay. The cobblestone streets were cold or hazardous or both and led directly to the Betsy Ross House. Who wanted to visit the Betsy Ross House? Even Chinatown was a cheat— two blocks long, three blocks wide, and a couple dead ducks hanging in a window. Philadelphia was in a dysfunctional funk. Desperate immigrants eschewed it like a border checkpoint.

If not for work or fun, why schlep to Stupidelphia?

Then something happened. Something huge. The date was the event: 9/11. Catastrophe changes everything, and as callous or ghoulish as it might sound, Philadelphia benefited enormously from the national tragedy. No one planned it that way, it just happened. Explosions to the north and the south and the west left Philadelphia unscathed, fairly glowing. All dangerousness was drained. It was out of harm's way. Al Qaeda turned Tioga toughs into teddy bears. The unintended consequence of being an insignificant city (or plum lucky) was the transformation of Philly into a sanctuary. The taint was suddenly the place to be, cuz. T'aint this target, t'aint that target, it's just the taint, the quaint taint, fortuitously floating under terrorist radar, conveniently located between two major bull's-eyes.

Philadelphia was finally seen by Americans for what it had been all along: close enough to anywhere, far enough from everywhere.

Comparisons to New York that had plagued the city for so long were suddenly turned upside down. Next to the gored Goliath, Philly was sweet David. Visiting Philadelphia became an oddly patriotic act. Tourism rose from 6.3 million people in 2000 to 8.3 million in 2004. More people saw the Liberty Bell last year than Yosemite National Park. Ground Zero remained too raw, too anxiety-provoking, an unmarked grave, a chasm in the American psyche. In the months and years after 9/11, every time a politician uttered the words "democracy" or "liberty"—most often referring to Iraq, which had its own particular visitation spike—they were subliminally advertising Philadelphia, the birthplace of that democracy, the cradle of that liberty. Every time the president stammered something about the "Constitution" in connection with the Patriot Act or tortured prisoners or Supreme Court nominees, it was a plug for Philadelphia, home of that Constitution.

Traipsing through historic Olde City was part of the national therapy. Regardless of cuisine, Philly restaurants were serving up comfort food. Cheesesteaks tasted like Norman Rockwell paintings. Betsy Ross was the girl across the aisle in elementary school. Citizens went straight from Carpenters' Hall to Home Depot. Mad props for tradition.

America was down so low that Philly looked like up. It had been reborn by being overlooked. And not just by terrorists, but by state-side disasters, natural and otherwise. No New Orleans floods, no LA earthquakes, no Texas border fights, no Chicago wind, no St. Helens volcanos, no Vegas debauchery, no Detroit crime, no AC casinos, no New England rains, no Florida hurricanes, no NYC prices, no DC scandals, and no Republicans in charge of anything. Spared by Allah and Mother Nature and Providence, Philly looked like the safest big city in America. The capital of the state of grace.

Tourists, business travelers, and parents who chaperoned their kids to Penn or Bryn Mawr or Moore College of Art would return to Anywhere, USA, and tell their friends and neighbors, "We just spent a weekend in Philadelphia. No, really. And it was a nice place. Lots of restaurants. Adorable brownstones and art galleries and cute cobblestone streets. The Art Museum in the evening, with the lights reflecting on the river, it was as dreamy as anything in Paris or Prague. We stayed at a lovely hotel on Rittenhouse Square. And nothing was expensive. Imagine—Philadelphia."

When they turned on NPR, they heard "From the WHYY studios in Philadelphia, I'm Terry Gross and this is *Fresh Air* . . ." What followed were interviews with Philip Roth or Richard Clarke or Keith Jarrett so sophisticated and empathic that Gross provided a sonic harbor in a sea of noise. *Fresh Air* aired every day, twice a day, and its adult attributes were subliminally grafted onto their city of origin. Radio Free Philadelphia, a beacon of civility and humor. (Didn't Garrison Keillor change your perception of Minnesota? Okay, Keillor plus Prince?) Philadelphia is mentioned at the top, middle, and end of every show. Multiply six times a day by 450 stations and you see how Terry Gross became the city's best ambassador since Ben Franklin, who, like Gross, was born

elsewhere. (Boston and Syracuse, respectively.) Even her musical inter-
ludes were tasty. Why not? She's married to Francis Davis, a home-
grown jazz historian, critic for the *Atlantic Monthly*, and author of
Bebop and Nothingness: Jazz and Pop at the End of the Century.

College kids with fresh diplomas figured out old factories made
cool lofts, vacant lots made great gardens, urban decay had its bright
side—small price tags. The brain drain was halted. When artists from
all over the country rolled into town, everything went from fucked-
up to fixer-upper. This was the last affordable metropolis on the East
Coast with all the amenities, diverse population, first-rate food, clubs,
bands, other artists, pro teams, and a gayborhood too (from Broad to
11th, from Chestnut to Pine).

Yo, Philly really wasn't half as bad as Philadelphians said it was.
And when *National Geographic Traveler* dubbed it "the next great
city," there was no turning back. And when PBS called it a wondrous
oasis, with the cleanest water, the most progressive WiFi mesh, and
the most artistic rejuvenation in the nation, it was official. Harry
Wiland, the producer of *Edens Lost and Found*, said flat-out: "If I were
twenty-five and a social activist, or an entrepreneur, or an architect, I
would move to Philadelphia. It is the most hopeful place in America.
It is small enough, concentrated enough, and positive enough to get
anything done."

Hot damn. Talk about a city reborn.

Filthydelphia morphed into Illadelphia, aka Funkadelphia, aka
P-Delphia, aka Chilladelphia. Despite the sensation, the change had
not happened overnight, only the revelation. While no one was paying attention, the old town had modernized and made itself present-
able. The foundation had been dug by Mayor Rendell's reverence for
the arts, by Jane Golden's modern frescoes, by David Dye's World
Café on WXPN, by the Green Plan that filled open spaces with beauty
and waters with health.

"Philadelphia: The City That Loves You Back" needed a quick
rewrite. It was an awful line from the get-go, and standard riffs

around the country were "Philadelphia: Watch Your Back" and "Philadelphia: Don't Come Back!" So ad folks came up with "More Fun When You Sleep Over." Hotels loved it, even if, or perhaps because, it sounded like an invitation to a pajama party or the title of a new Pink song. To tap into the burgeoning gay market, a separate million-dollar campaign was launched: "Get Your History Straight and Your Nightlife Gay." Television commercials showed a colonial dude rejecting the advances of a colonial wench and waltzing off with a guy in ponytail, breeches, boots, and ruffled shirt. Print ads featured saucy revolutionary lesbians and Ben Franklin flying a rainbow kite with a young pilgrim in tow.

Philly went a-courtin' and it worked. After San Francisco, it became the primary destination for gay tourists, who happen to spend twice as much as their straight counterparts.

When it's time for a new slogan, they might put this one in the suggestion box:

"See Our Crack by Day and Get Your Bell Rung at Night."

In my small, dark, $400 Ritz room, the light doesn't work and water barely trickles from the showerhead. The bellhop cannot fix the lamp or the shower. He offers to send an engineer. I ask about the noise from City Hall. He cannot stop that either, but guarantees the heavy construction will stop sometime during the night and resume early tomorrow morning. I pay him for all the information.

Not until you surf through all the channels do you realize how many movies Steven Seagal has made without your knowledge or approval. You want to watch the news, but the anchorwomen keep getting in the way. Robin Meade on CNN is dazzling. Laurie Dhue on Fox has lipo-lips that drip with gloss and reflect the klieg lights of the studio. She is not the kind of woman you want to ask, "What's new in the world?" She is the kind of woman you want to interrupt in mid-sentence and say, "Stop talking." Liz Cho is a model. More time has been spent sculpting her lustrous black tresses than her diction. She is such a delicious blend of so many ethnicities that you want to express your love of country by spooning from her melting pot.

These newswomen were apparently hired to distract you from the misery of the world. Or to save weary travelers money on the porn channels.

I call my wife. I get the voicemail greeting, my own voice. I hate my own voice. My wife must be out to dinner with a friend. Or maybe looking for a truant patient. Or walking the dog. I really don't know where she is. Or why people always guess where you are when you don't answer the phone.

"Hi," I say. "Everything is fine. The day went well. I'm at the Ritz and not long for this world. Talk to you tomorrow. Good night. Oh, I stopped by Hahnemann today. Big changes. Talk to you tomorrow."

My wife was studying psychology at Hahnemann when I met her. She is a New Yorker. Therapists from other cities, she told me, had a special challenge when treating natives, since Philadelphians were generally unhappy, and mildly happy about being generally unhappy, and suspicious of anyone, especially out-of-towners, who wanted to mess around with that balance. So visiting therapists were discouraged, not to say stymied. They couldn't tell if a patient was clinically depressed or just fifth-generation Fishtown. How could they decide whether to prescribe Prozac or prohibit a Phillies subscription package? When she told me that Freud merely hoped his patients would blossom into reasonably miserable humans, I told her therapists in Philly should be content with turning out grumpy, semiparanoid pricks who still see Frank Rizzo in their dreams but can actually make it to sessions on time, fully clothed, and are able to refrain from booing any observation she might make. If they pay, it's gravy. If they pay without complaint, she gets a statue next to Rocky.

I wake up in the middle of the night. I am having bad dreams of my own. Not about Rizzo or Rocky, but tourists, hordes of them, dressed like Mongol Mummers on dragon floats lip-synching "We've Only Just Begun" by the Carpenters. On a smaller, separate float,

Karen Carpenter is starving herself to death. I toss and turn until I dash off a letter on Ritz-Carlton stationery.

Dear Stephen Starr,

*Far be it from me to advise the most successful restaurateur in America, but I think I have stumbled upon a ripe notion for your empire. A hotel. On Broad Street. North of City Hall. Center City has hotels and Rittenhouse Square has hotels and Old City has hotels, but North Philly? Make it a boutique hotel if you must. With a fabulous restaurant, of course. You're a restaurant guy. Hell—**the** restaurant guy. The brightest Starr in the culinary galaxy. North Broad needs a restaurant as well. You can have your cake and sleep in it, too. You want to change a neighborhood, make a real contribution? You can fill two needs with one brilliant structure. You say you enjoy the design element more than the food—for which you bring in famous chefs—so why not go all design and open a hotel? Your friend David Rockwell will help.*

When someone in Logan has family visiting from North Carolina, where do they stay? Don't tell me the Ritz. Check out the letterhead. I know the Ritz. When a family in Olney has guests, where should they stay? Do not say the Four Seasons. You can help. There are no hotels on North Broad Street. Not in Olney, not in Tioga, not nowhere. Sure, there's a small motel near Temple University where no one stays unless they are being romanced by the football team. And that's always a short, bitter honeymoon.

I have some preliminary calculations. If you had a modest one-hundred-room hotel, and charged a modest $200 a night, in one year, you would see a modest $7 million from rooms alone. Add food, and parking, and stores, and other extras, and hot damn! Home run! And here's the best part of hotels: they raise their rates when their clientele needs them the most. That's right. If a hotel is nearly sold out on a Wednesday, for example, the price of the remaining rooms go sky-high, sometimes by 50 per-

cent or more. Like airplane seats, they make up the rates accord-
ing to the booking, the time of year, maybe even the weather. So a
$200 room gets jacked up to $250 or $300. I swear this is true.
The better you do, the more you charge. Sweet, huh? Like if one of
your restaurants was sold out on a Saturday night, or Valentine's
Day, you could raise the price of the $100 foie gras–truffle–
asiago–cheesesteak or double the price of your $230 Beaulieu
Vineyard Georges de Latour 2001 Cabernet Sauvignon.

Have I got your attention yet? I know how you work. Pedal to
the metal. Step on their throats when they are down!

It doesn't seem to hurt the hotel business.

Well, I have to try to go back to sleep now. Sleeping in hotels is
not easy. I know you'll do something about that.

> *Sincerely,*
> *Bruce the Bellhop*

P.S. By the way, your restaurant policy of not letting anyone sit
down at a table until the whole party arrives can be very irritat-
ing, and ought not be duplicated in the new NoBro Starr Bou-
tique Hotel. When someone needs some sleep, he needs sleep, and
can't be waiting for the rest of his party.

Next morning, I weigh myself in the bathroom. I love this Ritz-
Carlton scale. It says one day of a long walk on Broad Street will take
off thirty-five pounds. Flattery is fine, but keep it semireal. I leave the
faulty scale outside the door like a suit needing pressing. My neighbor
across the hall has not finished his room service breakfast. He wasn't
wild about the cheese Danish. It's not half bad.

On the second floor of the hotel is a business center where I check
my e-mails. Here's one from ol' Tom Ferrick.

Bruce,

I thought you were dead. You were so much older than the rest
of us.

I joke, of course.

I have been at The Inky since 1976 . . . a very long time . . . though only doing the column for six years. . . . It is the one way to make money in this business and not be an editor.

My boys are 12 and 16.

I walk Broad St. nearly every day.

When we were at Temple, people in the admin. really hated your writing. I guess it was your "No one ever accused Paul Anderson of being a bad ass motherfucker" lede.

But I liked it.

And it looks like you and me have made a life of writing, which is a good life.

> *—tf*

I reply:

Dear Ol' Tom Ferrick,

I am impressed that your long-term memory is functioning so well you can quote a lede from 35 years ago.

I am only one year older than you. But I forgot I even interviewed the president of Temple University or wrote about it in the Temple News.

I have two sons, 26 and 26. Twins.

When I die, you'll know it. A modest mural of me will be painted somewhere on Broad Street between your home and the Inquirer, so you can see me every day on your way to work. It should cost about $12,500. I'm saving my money. Given the choice between a satin deep-dish copper box at Goldstein Rosenberg Raphael-Sacks or a mural, I'm going for the wall every time.

I am asking other writers if they want a mural on the same street. The city can call it the Writer's Block. Wanna sign up now? Just send me a check.

As for this good writing life, it beats the alternatives.

SHARPSHOOTING KIDS

Ellsworth Street to Snyder Avenue

ONION, FRUIT OF GRACE
   by Julia Kasdorf, Philadelphia poet

Onion, fruit of grace
you swell in the garden
hidden as the heart of God,
but you are not about religion.
Onion, frying into all those Os,
you are a perfect poet,
and you are not about that.
Onion, I love you,
you sleek, auburn beauty,
you break my heart though
I know you don't mean
to make me cry.

Peeling your paper skin,
I cry. Chopping you,

I cry. Slicing off
your wiry roots,
I cry like a penitent
at communion, onion.
Tasting grace, layer by layer,
I eat your sweet heart
that burns like the Savior's.
The sun crust you pull on
while you're still underground,

I've peeled it.
Onion, I'm eating
God's tears.

WALKING to the Broad Street Diner at Ellsworth Street, I am surprised to find my body in a quiet condition. No barks or squeaks. These Mephistos must be excellent boots. The French can produce more than wine and ennui. I grab a *Daily News* as I enter the diner. New to the menu are the buffalo burgers ($3.95 or $5.95 deluxe) from the North Fork Bison Company, which guarantees no chemicals, hormones, steroids, or animal by-products; low in fat, calories, and cholesterol. Sounds healthy. I order scrapple, scrambled eggs, well-done homefries, toast, butter, and coffee. I will not be buffaloed by Ted Turner or any other ranchers. We have done enough damage to the bison.

A female police officer sits in a booth across the aisle. I nod in her direction before lowering my head into the *Daily News*.

There is a story about a young man and woman who just reached Tijuana after the first known trek down the Pacific coast. They walked 1,800 miles. 1,800 miles! They are smiling. Their names are Sarah and Nate. Sarah and Nate! What is this, a cruel joke? Those are the same names as the lead characters in my mother's joke. Only these are young folks, twenty-three and twenty-eight, who have just walked for three months across beaches and rain forests, through farm country and military bases, over sea walls and jetties, around contaminated rivers. They averaged twenty miles a day trekking from the giant redwoods of Washington state to the Mexican border near San Diego. They named the route they traversed: the West Coast Trail. Three months on the road and that's the best they can come up with?

It says Sarah is writing a book from the notes she kept along the way, and Nate posted a daily blog. Where did she buy pencils? Where did he power up his computer? I have scraps of paper with notes in my socks and my watch pocket, runic symbols scribbled on handouts from liquor stores and hairdressers, quotes from car towers and funeral directors and sock vendors in margins of newspapers, and Sarah and Nate kept dual diaries in backpacks? It says they met at the University of Georgia—Bulldogs—but it doesn't say if they are lovers or friends or exactly what they did on all those warm wet muddy nights on the hills and dales and forest floors. Can a man and a woman commune with nature for three months and not each other? Are Sarah and Nate crossing the border right now to score a kilo of Tijuana's finest in order to write their memoirs? I'd like to read about that.

My platter arrives with a slice of orange, a sprig of parsley, fluffy eggs, and scrapple so undeniable and so hot that it burns the skin off my tongue. The female cop is watching me as blood drips out of my mouth and onto my place mat. The place mat says: "Sliding into third base at age 43 wasn't so smart. Getting fixed up at Methodist Hospital was. Call 1-800-JEFF-NOW." Jeff-now? Methodist Hospital? Oh. Must be my old friend, the Thomas Jefferson Methodist Mercy St. Agnes Medical Center for Acute or Continuing Care. The cop watches my every move. She is eating a plain grilled cheese sandwich. She should try it with fried onions. I pick up my cell phone to call 1-800-JEFF-NOW now. I missed a call. It is not from the Lose Serious Weight people or the Earn Money At Home people, both of whom have somehow rejected me without ever speaking to me.

I try to keep in mind what my Buddhist monk/filmmaker son has told me: the first dharma lesson is to take nothing personally. Not the traffic, not global warming, not the waitress late with the coffee refill, not rejection from venal companies or treasured loved ones. The message on the phone is from my brother. He wants to know if I made it through North Philly unscathed and if I have, would I please pick him up a secondhand black Swedish Navy poncho at I. Goldberg, the best Army & Navy store in the country.

I call back and leave him a message: "The good news is that I am under the surveillance of a cop and bleeding only from my mouth. The bad news is that I. Goldberg has moved and is off limits for my Broad Street walk. Don't take it personally. Nothing works out the way you plan."

"Thank you for calling JEFF-NOW," says Jeff-now. "All representatives are currently assisting other callers. Please remain on the line and your call will be answered in the order it was received. Please become a Jefferson blood donor today. Call this number . . ."

More blood? More calls? What gives?

On my way out of the diner, I stop by the cop's table.

"You should try fried onions on your grilled cheese," I say.

"You should try fried eggs without blood," she says.

The JNA Institute of Culinary Arts is at Broad and Federal. JNA is a South Philly acronym for Joe and Anthony, the father and son who started the school. Today, Bob Fox answers phones, schedules students, and entertains guests all at the same time.

"Who pays more for a cantaloupe?" he asks. "A consumer or a restaurant?"

"Consumer," I say.

"Wrong. That's the hardest lesson for any student to learn—a restaurant pays more."

"Why?"

"They have the cantaloupes delivered, they get the best ones, they can rely on the freshness, they run a tab, they pay their bills late. All that costs money."

Chef Bob—that's what everyone calls him—went to Temple University, studied trumpet, and then worked at Odeon in New York for five years. His white double-breasted chef's jacket barely contains his appreciation of food. For a fine meal, he says, he would gladly spend a week's salary, and mentions Le Bec Fin, Django, Vetra, and the Four Seasons.

Though most of the eighty students at JNA are pros, few work at restaurants; schools, prisons, old age homes, institutions large and small. JNA caters to working stiffs. Chef Bob weeds out Main Line dilettantes who want to fork over a lot of dough so they can sneak in a few episodes of *Semi-Homemade Cooking* on the Food Network and crow about being JNA grads.

On the first floor of what appears to be a grand old movie theater, classes are held in the large and cushy lobby before moving into the huge stainless steel kitchen. Chef Bob hands out five pages to each student for immediate consumption. The handout contains the history of and recipes for—what else—the onion. A twenty-minute film is shown on the planting, growing, purchasing, and cooking of onions. Egyptians worshiped the onion in 3000 B.C. as a symbol of eternity. Ramses IV was entombed with onions in his eye sockets. Before Olympic games in ancient Greece, athletes had onions rubbed on their bodies, drank onion juice, and consumed pounds of the raw vegetable.

Two of the nine students are snoring before Jesus is born, but the wide-awake Kiesha, a thirty-year-old woman who works at a rehab center, when hearing that "onions lower cholesterol and blood pressure," vows that, from this day forth, she will feed her boyfriend only onions in order to cure his blood woes. Another student wonders aloud if Kiesha will try rubbing onion juice on certain muscles used in Olympic events.

Like truffles, a little knowledge goes a long way, and not always salutarily.

Classes can last three hours, depending on the dishes being prepared, so I decide to hit the street before the chopping of the onions begins.

In Manhattan, the constant swarm of buzzing people sets the pace. Move along or get froggered. It's always a mild assault and you have to keep awake. Residential SoBro is quieter, sparser, you can progress at your own rhythm, drink in the surroundings, listen to your own thoughts. One foot in front of the other, feel the concrete underfoot. Step on a crack, break your mother's back, step on a line, break your father's spine. Let the thoughts wash over you. Smell the fried onions. Remember Thich Nhat Hanh, the Vietnamese Buddhist monk who taught your sons his walking meditation at Plum Village in France, and how they, in turn, took their parents to Vermont to see the little man of great compassion. What you saw that first day were green mountainsides dotted with adult humans moving like zombies, trying to slow down their bodies and their minds.

You had to dial down your skepticism.

The silent meals reminded me, unhappily, of boarding school. At night, in our room, my wife refused to talk to me. Okay, it was a "silent week," but we were alone behind closed doors and there was much to talk about and we always shared a lusty mistrust of authority. I had questions. She had her index finger touching her pursed lips, followed by a waggling of that finger as she shook her head in bemused scorn.

Whispering, I read her the first doctrines from one of Thich Nhat Hanh's innumerable books:

"Do not be bound to any doctrine, theory, or ideology, even Buddhist ones . . ."

She waggled.

"Do not think that the knowledge you presently possess is changeless, absolute truth . . ."

She got into bed. Her bed. A futon.

"Do not force others, including children, by any means whatsoever, to adopt your views, whether by authority, threat, money, propaganda . . ."

She rolled over to stare at the wall.

" . . . or a silent treatment in the Green Mountains," I improvised.

When Thich Nhat Hanh entered the large tent early the next morning, it was the first time I'd ever seen him in person. He was tiny, delicate, unimposing. He sat on his folded legs and his expression was beatific. I wanted to kill him. Stab him through his brown robes with a sword. I don't know why. (Freudians, start your meters.) (On second thought, if they've been idle 'til now, don't bother.) On the spot, I guessed it was the threat he posed, his gentleness, his theft of my children, his muting of my wife, his living embodiment of the dedication I would never muster, the high and holy realms I would never reach, the bliss I would never know, the endless books of poetry and remembrances that I would never write. Maybe that's what my homicidal brothers felt when they saw Jesus or Gandhi or Martin Luther King. Envy is a deadly sin in any faith.

"If you meet the Buddha on the road, kill him." A Zen koan.

Here at Broad and Snyder is where the Fancy Mummers start their floats. Can't fit all twenty thousand Mummers on the same starting block, so the String Bands start at Oregon Avenue, south of here, and Comics at Broad and Washington, back a ways. The annual parade starts at 9 A.M. New Year's Day and ends when you pass out. It's the tradition, cuz.

All the Mummers—some wearing 150-pound jewel-encrusted, feather-loaded backpieces—strut the miles to City Hall to get judged in their divisions and polish off their flasks and, win or lose, head out for serious drinking with friends and eventually wind up on Two Street, capital of Mummerland, and get resmashed at the annual block party. It's the tradition, cuz.

And the tradition dates back to 400 B.C. when Roman peasants marched in masks at the festival of Saturn, celebrating the harvest and lampooning the wealthy politicos. Cut to medieval England: troupes of costumed performers went from house to house presenting a mummers play, or folk drama, around Christmas. In Philadelphia, in the 1700s, immigrant revelers welcomed the New Year by unloading their pistols into the sky. Groups of five or twenty, faces blackened for anonymity, strolled the streets reciting doggerel and receiving cakes and ale for their efforts. It was the one day a year where normal decent folk could dress up like women and clowns, could transgress taboos, could act out deep fantasies, turn the potentates into cartoons. Anyone and anything was fair game for burlesquing, including the newly inaugurated president, George Washington. One clown, Cooney Cracker, was so effective he became the model for Uncle Sam.

The first formal Mummers Parade was staged on January 1, 1901, and the Philly City Council appropriated $1,725 for prizes. The money is closer to $400,000 now, though no club makes a profit, and the event remains uncommercialized, if not unchanged. Mummers have gone through stretches of racism, sexism, alcoholism, thugism, xenophobism; strutting privileges were passed from generation to generation; clubs were restricted, women were banned, blackface was smiled upon. Tradition cuts both ways, cuz.

A couple years ago, all the tradition was halted—satire was suddenly out of bounds. Word got out that the Slick Duck Comic Brigade were to have cops chasing priests who were chasing altar boys while nuns danced in go-go cages. Cardinal Anthony Bevilacqua immediately called on all Catholics to "express their displeasure at the insensitive and tasteless skit." He said, "I am horrified that any person or group can be so callous. While such mean-spirited mockery may be protected as free speech, it is still hateful speech and as such has no place in a city parade."

The cardinal said nothing about grown men dressing up as cheerleaders, hunting dogs, cowgirls, nurses, prisoners, featherdusters, French maids, hobos, angels, devils, or donkeys.

Accustomed to such haranguing, the Slick Ducks let the threats roll off their backs; they were convinced the public needed an outlet for its revulsion at the nationwide scandal and they had the artistic license. Formal complaints were then lodged by the Archdiocese of Philadelphia; the Diocese of Camden, New Jersey; and the Catholic League. Mayor Street, mindful of the Catholic bloc, was forced to say he'd scuttle the skit if only he could. He couldn't. But, in the end, the leverage of the church and the government, coupled with the buckling of the local television station, conspired to sink the Slick Ducks. The skit was dropped from the parade. On Mount Olympus, Greek gods reached for their thunderbolts.

Alas, the cardinal was more offended by the Slick Ducks than sick priests. Two years later, a grand jury in Philadelphia concluded that at least sixty-three priests had sexually abused hundreds of boys and girls over the past decades. The jurors found the "cunning cover-up" by two archbishops as disturbing as any of the sadism unleashed on the kids. Those two were cardinals Anthony Bevilacqua and John Krol, who, the jury concluded, showed "utter indifference to the suffering of the victims" while putting the legal, financial, and moral reputation of the archdiocese ahead of protecting the children entrusted to its care.

Led by Bevilacqua, the church attacked the grand jury as it had the Slick Ducks, calling it anti-Catholic and wrapping itself in compassion for the priests, not the victims.

Just thinking about the cardinals and the Mummers puts a slight strut in my step. Mummers never march, they strut. As do all Philadelphians when they are feeling frisky. It's in the DNA. You slouch some, hang your arms loose and wide, like a blue heron preparing for take-off, flap your wings, bend your knees, and cakewalk, on your toes, chest out, head bobbing high and hard and insouciant all at the same time, like you're building up to do whatever it is you are about to do. You never strut a straight line—you serpentine, some forward and then back, sideways and in circles. And you start to hear yourself humming "O, Dem Golden Slippers." You can't help yourself. You don't want to.

Ms. Florence Giannini greets every customer who enters the Wachovia Bank at Broad and Porter. She has been sitting here, on her stool, for fourteen years, even though the name of the bank has changed five times in that period. In one long sentence, without notes, Ms. Giannini will tell you how she started with Central Penn that soon became American that was bought by Meridian that was taken over by Core States that was purchased by First Union that merged with Wachovia. Wachovia is new in town, and quite serious: it has plastered its name everywhere, most notably on the arena where the 76ers and Flyers perform. Wachovia is a bastardization of the German name Wachau (rhymes with Dachau). When German settlers arrived in North Carolina in the 1700s, the land reminded them of a valley along the Danube River called Die Wachau. Thus Wachovia.

Florence Giannini, South Philly native, chatty and efficient, knows a thing or two about banking evolution and surviving corporate upheaval.

"Yes, banking has changed," she says.

"How so?" I ask.

"Please don't quote me," she says.

"Why not?" I ask.

"I don't want to get in trouble with Wachovia."

"All you said was banking has changed."

"That's right. Banking used to be snobby. It's more friendly now. That's why I'm talking to you."

"Thank you."

"But don't quote me," she says.

"I am thinking of quoting you, Florence," I say.

"Why?"

"You're one of the sweetest people I have ever met."

"There are eighteen banks in a one-mile radius," says Florence, with new earnestness, "and I never forget the only thing that separates us from all the rest is our service. We don't give you a refrigerator when you open an account anymore. Those days are long gone. We don't give away anything. Banking has changed a lot. And more than just the names."

"Whatever happened to Girard Bank?" I ask.

"Girard became Mellon and Mellon became Citizens," says Florence. "They have a stadium too."

Florence refers to Citizens Bank Park, home of the Phillies, right next to Lincoln Financial Field, home of the Eagles. Banks and professional sports deserve each other. You can't afford a ticket without stopping at an ATM.

At Broad and Shunk, right between Laval's LaserLight Based Photoepilation and Superior Physical Therapy, Inc., is the U.S. Army recruiting office. You can spot it by its distinctive black and yellow logo. What happened to camouflage and olive green? Imagine combing the backstreets of Tikrit in black and yellow. Soldiers, decked out in sand-colored Star Wars outfits, might think the Pittsburgh Steelers are running interference.

"I believe those are just colors for advertising," says Sergeant First Class Cristifaun Moore. "If you want more information, you have to contact PAO."

Sergeant Moore, from North Carolina, has a most pleasant way of not answering questions. She assures me the Army brochure will provide all the necessary information. On the cover is the "Army of One" logo. And you thought the Army was built around teamwork. Inside are four-color photographs of soldiers: thirty-six Caucasians, eight African-Americans, and two Asians (one a doctor).

Sergeant Moore is the person you want captured in the Sunni Triangle, not in South Philly. She is tight-lipped and close-mouthed. She deflects every query with the suggestion that I get in touch with PAO. Finally, I give in.

"Okay, Sergeant Moore, I'll talk to PAO," I say.

"That would be advisable," she says.

"What is PAO?"

"Public Affairs Office," she says.

Captain Lidia Weatherspoon heads the local PAO.

"Black and yellow is strictly for advertising," she says. "Anything else?"

"Army of One," I say.

"The intention was to say 'You are a soldier, you count, and the sum is no greater than its parts.' Army of One means teamwork, but people misunderstand it, think it's the opposite. It might be confusing. Anything else?"

"You getting recruits from the Broad Street station?"

"South Broad Street is a small station. Not much action."

"How did you pick South Broad Street?" I ask.

"We put stations in areas where the demographics show a population with a propensity to join. Taken into consideration is age, income, education, family history. Far too complicated for us, so U-SARC farms it out to civilian companies who tell us where we should open stations."

"U-SARC?" I ask.

"U-SARC is the United States Army Recruiting Company."

"And the civilians told you South Broad Street would be productive?"

"We have to beat the streets to get recruits everywhere in Philadelphia," says Captain Witherspoon.

"Beat the streets?"

"We have a big challenge in Philadelphia," she says.

"What's the problem, Captain?"

"The Philadelphia school system," she says.

"What's wrong?"

"Talking to my colleagues and counterparts across the country, Philadelphia schools are, overall, well, not very good. Not on par with other regions."

"How can you tell?"

"Army applicants have to pass a written exam before taking the physical or moral tests, and Philadelphia doesn't cut it. That first hurdle is too high for a lot of Philly kids."

"How difficult is the test?" I ask.

"It's an eighth-grade-level test for math and English. And a lot of high school graduates from Philadelphia can't pass it."

"Come again," I say. "Kids with a Philadelphia high school diploma fail the Army's eighth-grade math exam?"

"Other areas don't have that problem," she says. "Even in the same state—not in the suburbs or the rural areas. Not in Coatesville, for one example."

(Of the 660 public high schools in Pennsylvania, forty of the bottom hundred are in Philly. Of the worst fifty, eighteen are in Philly.)

In Coatesville, Pennsylvania, the Army recruiting office beat last year's total and reached this year's goal with plenty to spare. Sure, they offer up to $15,000 per soldier and bring in veterans of the Iraq and Afghanistan conflicts (wars? incursions? liberations? civil wars?) to tell nifty war stories and spread rah-rah reassurances. Drugs are not a problem. Before a recruit goes for a physical, the local recruiter administers a preliminary drug test, and if the recruit fails, he or she is told to clean up and come back another day. There are no limits on how many times a potential recruit can be "dirty"—Army parlance—and come back a week or two later.

"Maybe you're administering the wrong test," I say.

"What do you propose we do?"

"Doesn't the Army need sharpshooters?" I ask.

"Yes."

"Maybe you should get the Philly kids out of the classroom and onto the rifle range. Young Philadelphians are excellent with firearms. They lead the nation in killing other kids—thirty kids killed in 2003, twenty-seven more kids in 2004. Over half with firearms. Now, that's pretty good shooting."

"This is no joke," says Captain Weatherspoon.

"Nothing funny about it. Of the forty-five kids who were killed in 2005, thirty-six of them were shot to death. That's no joke."

"Anything else?" she asks.

"Ever think Philadelphia kids are just stupid enough to be smart?"

"Excuse me?"

"Considering what's happening in the Middle East and all, failing an eighth-grade math test doesn't seem so dumb."

The conversation fizzles out from there. I don't have time to bring up the soldier who had his cousin shoot him in the leg so he wouldn't go back to Iraq. Specialist Marquise Roberts, twenty-three, of the Third Infantry, first told police that he had been wounded in his left leg when he strolled past two men arguing on a North Philly street corner. An investigation proved otherwise. And not high-class sleuthing, either. Police found no .22 caliber bullet casings, no blood, and no witnesses at the site of the alleged incident. On the hospital admittance report, Specialist Roberts said he was unintentionally dinged, wrong place, wrong time. His cousin, Roland Fuller, said the shooting took place when Specialist Roberts bravely tried to foil an attempted robbery, and then offered graphic details. Bing and bang. Two stories so spectacularly different you are almost glad Specialist Roberts is not returning to Iraq as a supply specialist. Didn't he anticipate some basic questioning by the admitting doctor, not to mention the police or his Army superiors?

Once the truth was out, the soldier's family members explained that Roberts had been, during his two-week holiday, terribly distraught, drinking heavily and crying and reliving his part in the bloody fall of Baghdad, how he had been on the front lines for seven months, had served his country admirably, had seen too many friends die, and how his Army stint had not worked out the way he planned. He was not going back to Iraq.

And so it came to pass. He is serving one year at Fort Bragg, North Carolina, for conspiracy, recklessly endangering another person, and filing a false police report. He faces possible court-martial. Roland Fuller, additionally charged with aggravated assault and weapons offenses, was sentenced to fifteen to thirty months in prison to be followed by two years' probation. His wife, Donna Fuller, pleaded guilty to carrying a firearm in public, criminal conspiracy, and criminal solicitation, and was sentenced to two to twenty-three months in jail, to be followed by four years' probation.

Fellow soldiers had strong opinions about the cousins on a Web site called GruntsMilitary.com.

o3shooter writes:

It would appear that some sorry supply puke just got his cousin to shoot him in the leg so that he wouldn't have to go back to Iraq. I say that we should stand him up in front of a wall and FINISH THE JOB!!!

R/Pingjocky says:

What a dirt bag! From reading the story, I can plainly see that they made two mistakes:

1. They used the wrong caliber pistol . . . should have used a .45 instead of a .22.
2. They hit the wrong location . . . should have put the round in his head instead of the leg. That would have prevented him from going back to the war!

AFJim E-4 asks:

What kind of moron shoots himself to avoid being shot at? Hmm . . . get shot in battle, come home a hero. No screw that, I want to shoot myself and be known as a complete ass! Well, he will have some time to think about that decision in Leavenworth:

UCMJ Article 115—Malingering

Intentional self-inflicted injury in a hostile fire pay zone or in time of war. Dishonorable discharge, forfeiture of all pay and allowances, and confinement for ten years.

He gets my vote for Idiot of the Year! I'm surprised he didn't videotape it and send it in to MTV's *Jackass*. You gotta love my generation!

Pentagon officials say they cannot recall another instance of a soldier deliberately harming himself to avoid returning to the Middle East. But more than eight thousand members of the all-volunteer military have been charged with desertion since the invasion of Iraq in 2003. And thousands more failed to comply with orders to report for posting to Iraq or Afghanistan when called back to duty under the Individual Ready Reserve program.

No kids left to serve.

Across the street from the Army, Addus Health Care is in the business of providing nurses and nursing aides for the sick and elderly. Bernice Drinks runs the show. She sends out a hundred women, half of whom are immigrants, Latina, European, and Caribbean. For $16 an hour, they will do laundry, light cleaning, some cooking, run errands, help with ablutions, and act as companions. Registered nurses do more and cost more. Bernice Drinks plays it close to the vest.

"We've spoken before," I say.

"We have?"

"About my mother."

"What's your mother's name?"

"Rose Buschel."

Bernice Drinks's smile is unaccompanied by words.

"You remember her?" I ask.

"Maybe yes, maybe no. That's confidential," she says.

"She's passed away."

"I'm sorry," she says. "It's still confidential."

"I remember Chareeka," I say.

Chareeka was the woman who called me when my mother tried to kill herself.

After the false broken neck incident, after returning from McGee Rehab, my mother needed twenty-four-hour attention, more a collaborator than caregiver. Rita had been there for five years, had seen my mother's descent, and was, in many ways, my mother's closest confidant. But Rita had nursing school and a husband and could dedicate just so many hours. She helped interview and hire other women, overnighters and weekenders. Difficult was the task of finding suitable women for the support team. My mother didn't like heavyset women or accented women or gum-chewing women or overly talkative women or women who cleaned the kitchen floor without getting down on their hands and knees.

We ransacked Elder Care, Women's Medical, Epicare, JEVS, Addus. I had their phone numbers on speed dial. They knew my voice, or my name. Some of them hung up when they heard my voice, or my name. I used to think my mother's poster was hanging on all the agency walls above the phone.

If you suspect I may be exaggerating, may not be objective in these matters, these are the notations Rita kept about the women who came and went:

Rochelle: Rose called her Crazy Hair; she talks too much and too loud; she quit after two months.

Ruby: Looks like a man was Rose's complaint; kept hitting herself in the head with her hand because her weave was too tight.

Christina: Rose fired her after parole officer called to find out how she was doing on her new job.

Jane: Very nice; quit because she can't stand Rose constantly scratching her dry skin.

Teena: Rose asked for a glass of water and Teena said she would get it when she wanted, maybe tomorrow, maybe sometime in the future.

Edna: A Jamaican. Rose couldn't understand a word out of her mouth.

Cynthia: Walked around talking into her cell phone; she quit and was fired the same day.

Katrina: Said Rose treated her like a dog, and she quit the second week.

Ava: Very nice; said Rose was too hard a case.

Sheena: Rose told her to leave; Sheena wouldn't leave Rose alone in the apartment; Rose called security in the building and said Sheena was trespassing; Sheena said she was doing her job; police arrived; Sheena left.

Linda: Rose thinks Linda's cold made her sick and put her into the hospital and fired her when she visited.

Iridia: On her second day, called to say she would be late; Rose said don't bother coming back at all.

Lynnae: Eats all day, but never with Rose.

Liz: Quit; can't take the secondhand smoke.

Qeevon: Rose said not intelligent enough.

Marena: Wouldn't go to the store and just sat in the living room.

Shereen: After three days, she said she was ready to jump out of window; walked out the front door instead.

Daneen: Boyfriend snuck in at night when Rose was asleep.

Sereena: Rose doesn't like her and says checks were missing.

Regina: Worked one week, found out she's pregnant and doesn't feel well enough to return.

There was also Fifi, Charmaine (too old), Stacy, Ramona (Stacy's mother-in-law), Margaret, Debbie (too weak), Maria, Betty, Danielle, Dorothy, Kate (too fat), Blanche, and Chareeka.

It was Chareeka who called me one morning.

"Your mother," she said.

"Yes, what?"

"She took an overdose."

"Of what?"

"The Restoril," she said.

"How is she?"

"She's not moving. I think maybe . . . you should come."

"Is she breathing?"

"Yes."

"How many pills did she take?"

"The whole vial."

"How many were in there?"

"I think maybe twenty. I'm not sure."

"Call an ambulance and I'll leave now."

"One more thing."

"Yes."

"She left you a note."

My mother had had trouble sleeping. A doctor had prescribed Restoril. Medicines were never a problem to obtain. If she needed Valium, she made one phone call and a boy from the drugstore would deliver a hundred of them within an hour. Why an octogenarian with a history of depression would need a hundred Valium was never considered by the pharmacist. Her medicine cabinet had two dozen vials of pills and capsules, plus ointments and syrups, prescribed by no fewer than fifteen different physicians. The doctors' names were Indian, Chinese, Jewish, Irish, male, female, pronounceable and unpronounceable; they were names of interns, ER docs, internists, shrinks, cardio people, neuro folks, a skin specialist, one woman doctor who made house calls, and my brother—he sent blue-green algae every month.

From 1994 to 2001, my mother had survived a stroke, seizures, skin cancer, high blood pressure, failed kidneys, dialysis, depression, hair loss, constipation, atrial fibrillation, psoriasis, heart failure, and a broken knee. She spent time in four hospitals, three rehab facilities, and one geriatric psychiatric ward, twice. My mother had insurance from AARP and a backup health provider. She cost the system a bundle. Sometimes her hospital bills would read: "Total . . . $32,500. You pay . . . $24.85."

Wobbly at best, after taking Restoril to get to sleep, she could not keep her balance in the middle of the night or early the next morning. It was a powerful drug and too much for her 110 pounds. She fell five times in one month, like a baby, rarely getting hurt; she was frail but not fragile. Lucky too. Then came the misdiagnosed broken neck. After returning from rehab, she was thin and miserable and I fiddled with the contents of each Restoril, leaving maybe a quarter of the crystals in each capsule for the weight and some minimal potency. When my mother had prescriptions refilled, I asked Rita to do the same. Rita knew everything.

The placebo was not totally ineffective but lacked the knockout punch. My mother complained about not sleeping well, but that was nothing new. We tinkered with the crystals, adding, subtracting, arriving at a safe and moderate level. She stopped falling. It worked well enough and we got a kick out of finally pulling some wool over my mother's peering eyes, until, that is, she swallowed a whole vial's worth.

When I arrived at her apartment, I read her suicide note, its main focus being to disallow certain nurses from sitting on the sofa in the living room because they had greasy hair and would ruin the fabric. Someone might want the sofa after she was gone. Not much else. The lack of touching prose did little to stanch my cataract of emotion. My mother slept until noon and then awoke and wondered what had gone wrong with her plan. She thought, but wasn't sure, that she had taken a lot of sleeping pills, enough to end it all. She was groggy and incommunicative. She was confused and then embarrassed and angry. Angry at me, either intuitively or because she knew.

It was her death I had stolen. I felt guilty that I had, unintentionally, saved her life. I was trying to keep her from falling, not prevent her great escape. I kept imagining what she had gone through, yesterday and all the days before that, to arrive at that moment of writing the note and filling the glass and swallowing the pills. What hell. What relief that must beg for. I couldn't tell her what had happened, that her plan was fine, that I had undermined her bravest act. I felt too guilty. Still do. I was sorry. Still am. Wanting to keep her safe from falling into the downward spiral of hospital life, I pushed her into a private spiral of suffering.

She entered the hospital on September 12, 2001. I visited her there twice. Then she passed away, in her sleep, in her apartment, on October 3. She never knew about 9/11. There is odd comfort in that.

The end of Broad Street is getting near. I find myself darting to the finish line. Whoa. Slow down, dude. Deep breath. Why the anxiety? Endings? Indeed. You hate endings. Watch your thoughts flow. WWBD? Any Buddha outside yourself, on any road, is a trick Buddha and has to be eliminated. It's only the longing you have for Buddha. Everything has an ending. They are all heartbreaking. Your father's heart broke, stopped beating. These thoughts will end. The beat will stop.

Step on a crack, break your mother's back. Step on a line, everything is fine.

The Buddha you meet might be the Buddha that is yourself, and you must be free of that Buddha too. All things pass. If you are lucky enough to see your self outside yourself, in any form, teachers, squirrels, sadness, tailors, Army deserters, let it go, let it go. If you don't know you are the Buddha, then you'll have contempt for yourself and you naturally want to destroy all things contemptible. Sure. But you still hate endings. Your strut is long gone. Damn dem golden slippers.

Step on a crack, break your mother's back. Step on smack, you have more smack.

A homeless man is curled up in the doorway of a church just off Oregon Avenue. I assume he is homeless because he is fast asleep in the broad daylight, wrapped in a thick, holey blanket, in the fetal position. He has a beard that would be unwelcome in most office settings. He may have a home and opted not to stay there last night, or last week. Maybe his wife is driving him nuts. Stories can get strange. Or maybe he is waiting for the church to open so he can perform his duties as the janitor or the minister for the congregation at this Church of Jesus Christ of Latter-day Saints. Maybe he's a saint. Broad Street has seen its fair share of saints. I don't want to wake him and ask him. Even saints need their sleep. Maybe the man is a Mormon, and if he has been to Salt Lake City, he would have happened across State Street, which runs some twenty miles, and is considered by many to be the longest straight street in the world. Because it leaves the city and joins the desert, it doesn't qualify in my book.

If this man is from Russia, he might tell you that Moskovskaya Street in Saratov is, in fact, the longest straight street on earth. He won't say just how long. Russians are like that. They keep secrets. They can't help themselves.

No one argues that Yonge Street, at 1,195 miles, is not the longest known road, but it starts in Toronto and turns into Highway 11 and ends somewhere in North Ontario, where Neil Young was helpless, helpless, helpless, helpless. At twenty-six miles, Colfax, in Denver, may be the longest continuous street in America, but it's a highway that goes through four cities, Aurora, Denver, Lakewood, and Golden. Two Western Avenues are longer than Broad Street. The one in Chicago is twenty-four miles and straight as an arrow; the one in Los Angeles is twenty-three miles. (Sunset Boulevard runs for twenty-two miles, but has curves like a starlet.)

On foot, you can walk straight through City Hall without ever veering left or right, the courtyard serving as a tunnel; in a car, however, you have to drive around the ornate building, and sticklers claim Broad Street is therefore less than straight and true. In the end—the holy end!—Broad Street will settle for being the concrete spine of the city, the unswerving protector of all shakras, the uncrackable safety depository of a lifetime of memories. What's wrong with that?

1 4

BOOBIRDS OF HAPPINESS

Packer Avenue to the Navy Yard

LEAVES OF GRASS (excerpt)
   by Walt Whitman

I know I have the best of time and space,
and was never measured, and never will be measured.
I tramp a perpetual journey—(come listen all!)
My signs are a rain-proof coat, good shoes, and a staff cut from the
woods;

No friend of mine takes his ease in my chair;
I have no chair, no church, no philosophy;
I lead no man to a dinner-table, library, or exchange;
But each man and each woman of you I lead upon a knoll,

My left hand hooking you round the waist,
My right hand pointing to landscapes of continents,
and a plain public road.
Not I—not any one else, can travel that road for you,

You must travel it for yourself.
It is not far—it is within reach;
Perhaps you have been on it since you were born,
and did not know;
Perhaps it is every where on water and on land.
Shoulder your duds, dear son, and I will mine,
and let us hasten forth,
Wonderful cities and free nations we shall fetch as we go.

T A L K of the Town is a hole-in-the-wall hoagie joint under the
entrance to the Walt Whitman Bridge near the sports stadia
with the bank names. Inside Talk of the Town, headshots of
ballplayers cover the walls above the doors, those with live arms and
dead, sunny futures and sordid pasts, Philadelphia athletes who
won't make you too upset to eat. Behind the counter, an attractive
woman with an extra unbuttoned button on her blouse and a magi-
cal pushup-bra, looks up and asks, "What can I get ya, honey?"

You like being called honey.

"Chicken cheesesteak, please, peppers and fried onions."

"Is that all, sweetie?" You like being called sweetie.

The Hooters are on the radio. You miss Philly music. Philly
cheesesteaks. Philly women talking Philly smack. Why did you ever
leave? Could you handle this again? It feels so comforting, so melancholy. Feels like home. And you've never been here before. Tug McGraw
stares down from above. Billy Wagner has no reason to smile. You sit
down to rest your weary dogs.

"Chicken cheese!" You hop to attention.

"Here you go, sweetheart." You like being called sweetheart.

You begin to flirt with the idea that it's somewhat personal until the
woman with the unbuttoned third button and the push-up bra ad-
dresses the next guy in line, a linebacker of a truck driver with a
black Eagles cap who hasn't showered or shaved in days, maybe a

week. "What'll it be, sweetie?" she asks him and winks. He gets a wink?

Your sandwich suddenly goes limp and tasteless. The roll is soggy and the chicken too clucky and the whole thing falls apart halfway through. A lapful of fried onions. Maybe that's what you get for ordering a chicken cheesesteak instead of the real thing. The truck driver with the Eagles cap sits down next to you with his genuine cheesesteak and a *Daily News*.

"Almost time for them Iggles," he says, without looking up.

"You like their chances?" I ask.

"Tough team, good coach," he says.

"They goin' all the way?" I ask.

"That's the question, ain't it," says the truck driver.

"That's always the question," I say.

The truck driver smells stronger than his cheesesteak with hot peppers, onions, mushrooms, oregano, and tomato sauce.

"Dude lands in Hades," he says. "And the devil don't like the look of him, so he makes him break rocks with a sledgehammer. And just to be a prick, he cranks up the temperature. Next day, the devil checks in on this guy and he can't believe his eyes. He's swinging this big ol' sledgehammer and whistling a happy tune.

"Devil says, 'You're crushing rocks and I turned up the heat. Why so happy?'

"'Reminds me of an August day back in Philly,' says the guy.

"The devil is pissed. He drops the temperature below zero and plays tricks with the windchill. Suddenly, hell is three feet in snow and hot ice. The guy from Philly is dancing and singing and twirling his sledgehammer like a baton.

"Devil says, 'How can you be so happy? Don't you know it's 40 below zero?'

"The guy looks at the devil and says, 'If hell's freezing over, it can only mean one thing—the Eagles have won the fuckin' Super Bowl!'"

The truck driver returns to his cheesesteak and his *Daily News*.

Make no mistake, the Iggles are a religion around here and they put their congregants through hell. There are fundamentalist baseball believers and diehard hoopsters and hockeyheads, but everyone knows the Iggles are the dominant sectarian force. You will see more green in Philly than Dublin, jerseys, knit hats, jackets, windbreakers, banners, flags, tattoos, car decals. No one is immune. Not Charlotte Noteboom, who will spend her eternity at the midfield stripe at Lincoln Field. Her good son Christopher knew that his mom would be much happier at the Eagles games than sitting on his mantelpiece, so one Sunday, Charlotte's forty-four-year-old offspring darted across the green turf in his gray sweatshirt just before the second half kickoff against the Packers, said a Hail Mary, and emptied his mother's ashes from a plastic Baggie between the 30- and the 50-yard lines before falling to his knees, crossing himself, and praying not to be gang-tackled by the security force; sprinkling unknown white powder in the midst of fifty thousand Americans is frowned upon these days. The fans, however, savvy to the Eagles' sketchy running game, wanted the chunky Christopher Noteboom tendered a contract on the spot. A twenty-yard gain is a twenty-yard gain.

The Eagles have not won a championship since 1960. The Flyers not since 1975. The Phillies won one World Series in the last century. The Sixers own the newest crown in town, circa 1983. That's a total of 126 sports seasons without a championship. That's a long time. Odds-defyingly long time. Even those agnostics who initially scoffed at the notion of the "Curse of Billy Penn" are beginning to entertain the possibility. It started with the blueprints, not even the construction, of One Liberty Place in 1984, the first building to reach higher than Penn's pilgrim hat—sixty-one stories. Within a year, the Flyers lost their great goaltender, Pelle Lindbergh, in a car accident, and it's been one crash after another ever since. For some, Philly-bred Smarty Jones was the proof in the pudding. After winning the Kentucky Derby and the Preakness handily, mightily, he lost the Triple Crown by one cursed length at the Belmont. As for Barbaro, the Philly-owned phenom, RIP.

Edmund Bacon is chortling in heaven. On a skateboard.

After so many decades of brutal losses, it is possible that Philadelphians have become so used to anguish that winning is a frightening and foreign prospect. Identities are stubborn buggers, and not slipped into and out of like Victoria's Secret nightgowns. As much as Philadelphians complain, they love to complain, and commiserate, and drink themselves into justifiable stupors; stories about losing cut so much deeper than the alternative. Shakespeare ain't Shakespeare 'cause of the comedies.

Believers in reincarnation think there is something holy about being reborn a Philadelphian. You must have a lot of penance to pay, karma to burn, and you get to watch some unfuckingbelievably torfuckingmenting sporting events that you can pass along to your grandchildren, along with the unused 1964 Phillies World Series tickets.

Maybe local racetracks should pay out for Place, Win, and Show.

Philly fans are acknowledged as the least gracious, most vociferous, and most sadistic fans on earth. (Unless you count Uday Hussein's clandestine torture of soccer players when Iraq didn't reach the '94 World Cup Finals. Philly fans, need it be said, would rather boo than torture. Booing is more socially acceptable. Booing makes spectator sports participatory. Booing relieves the blues. Booing restores the delusion of influence over outcomes. The boobirds of happiness are happy to boo.)

It's true, they pelted Santa Claus. When Philadelphians see a skinny Santa in a lopsided beard and lumpy stuffing zigzagging across a frosty football field in an inebriated manner in the midst of a brutal losing streak, they do not cheer. They boo. And then pelt the sonuvabitch with snowballs. Iceballs if available. That's fun. Good clean sick Philly boobird fun. You want blind acceptance, send your pixilated Santa to St. Louis, where they cheer any schmuck in a red costume. You want partisan cheering, send Santa to DC, where they don't know lobbying from love. You trot someone, anyone, saint or sinner, before a Philadelphia crowd and you can rely on an instinctive and honest assessment. Not polite, but not fraudulent. Affection must be earned. Illusion will never find you at a Philadelphia sporting event. Even the favorite hometown soda is called Frank's.

Matthew Scott was the first person in America to receive a hand transplant. Advising him to throw out the first pitch at a Phillies home opener in 2002 was akin to sending Barbara Streisand out to sing the Kurdish National Anthem at a Sunni v. Shia soccer match. Perversity of the highest order. You think poor Matthew was unaware of the difference between bowling and baseball when his toss dribbled across home plate? You think he was oblivious to the dark humor of the situation? If he were, the fans enlightened him. Sure, booing the poor kid may have been in poor taste, but so poor that it was funny. Just because you get a new hand doesn't mean you get a big hand from Philly fans. Outsiders just can't grasp the fans' sophisticated humor, can't appreciate the perspicacity.

Blame Momus, the Greek god of satire and mockery. Momus won't mind being blamed. His name means blame and censure, and he is the patron god of Philly in whose name the Mummers were born. Momus lifts the masks from the overly pious and the hypocritical. Every Philadelphian has a little Momus inside waiting impatiently to boo. And then strut.

Yo, Philly fans can cheer too. They applaud hard work and dirt-encrusted uniforms. They applaud men sacrificing their bodies and statistics for the good of the team. They applaud when a Dallas Cowboys wide receiver is sprawled out on the field with a broken neck. How were they supposed to know it was a career-ending injury for Michael Irvin? You don't understand how much Eagle fans hate the Cowboys. The Cowboys can be detestable. The Cowboys are an archrival, as are the Giants and the Redskins and a couple other teams too. But the Cowboys had been cruisin' for a bruisin' since they appointed themselves America's Team. America this! Philly is as American as any city, and more than most. Malik Rose, homeboy, Drexel grad, NBA player, owner of Philly's Phamous cheesesteaks in San Antonio, put it this way: "We may boo Santa Claus and throw batteries in the end zone, but we don't throw $7 beers. We don't waste those."

The history of this sort of behavior started long before football or basketball went pro, back in 1920, when the Kessler brothers, Bull and Eddie, would station themselves on opposite sides of the Baker Bowl, one behind first and one behind third, and heckle the hell out of the Philadelphia Athletics.

A's manager-owner Connie Mack tried to nip this in the bud by taking the Kessler brothers to court. Mack lost. Free speech won. Then Mack tried to bribe the Kesslers with season passes if they'd only shut up. But Heckle and Jeckle, who sold fruit and vegetables from a pushcart, were having too much vituperative fun.

Before Herbert Hoover attended a Cards-A's World Series game in 1930, no president had ever been booed at a nonpolitical event. When throwing out the first pitch, 32,000 A's fans let him have an earful. The president thought they were booing his Great Depression. By the fourth inning, it became clear the crowd had other deprivations on their mind. "We want beer!" they chanted. "We want beer!" It was Prohibition that riled them.

The A's won that series in six games. They appeared in nine World Series and were world champions five times. They were the most successful sports franchise in the history of Philadelphia. And then they left in 1954. Just like that. Not for the Gold Coast or the Redwood Forests or the Gulf Stream waters, but for Kansas City. Kansas City!

Leave here, you are dead to us.

It didn't take long for all remnants of the A's to disappear. No one sports a retro A's cap or wears a Jimmie Foxx jersey. No one even talks about the A's. New Yorkers still pine for the Giants. Brooklynites still plot the return of their Dodgers. Baltimoreans feel for their Colts. The Philadelphia fan, with his elephant memory, has long ago buried the A's and their elephant logo. No franchise has ever been so thoroughly scrubbed from the blackboard of collective consciousness.

When Connie Mack Stadium was destroyed in 1976, so were the final vestiges of his legacy. Connie Mack is now a politician in Florida. The A's are a team with funny-colored uniforms in Oakland. Screw 'em.

You can see the four sports stadia from Broad Street. The urge overwhelming to sneak a peek at Citizens Bank Park, the Phillies' new home, I break my own rules and take a detour down Pattison Avenue. No games mean virtually no human traffic. You can't call me a fan anymore, not since I realized no scourge is visited upon the man who no longer roots for a group of strangers playing ball in the town where he grew up. We have all become mercenaries.

Passing Wachovia Center, formerly First Union Spectrum, formerly Core States Spectrum, brings to mind not basketball or hockey, but capitalism and bank mergers. You'd think financial institutions would be more stable. I have no desire to see the statue of Dr. J but I do remember hearing about it from the last athlete I admired in Philadelphia, the most ruminative jock I ever met. Mike Schmidt was in the twilight of his career when we spoke and wore the crown, uneasily, of greatest third baseman of all time.

"I haven't been booed for two years," he said. "And I don't know why." He was dead serious. The matter of booing had obsessed him since he arrived in Philadelphia.

I told him about the father and son I sat next to one game.

"Who are they booing, Dad?" asked the seven-year-old.

"See that man with curly hair and surly demeanor? That's the greatest third baseman in the history of baseball. That's who they're booing."

"But why, Daddy?"

"Even the great ones get booed, Son."

"Why is that?"

"Love is complicated. You can hit forty home runs a year, but if you strike out with the bases loaded, you hear about it. Same in life. You can arrive on time for dinner 350 days in a row—but show up late once, and your mother will nail you to the wall. Trust me. Love is complicated."

Schmidt didn't laugh.

"If a guy's gotta go to 500 home runs and get three MVPs just to stop getting booed," he said, "that's pretty sad, isn't it? They put up a fuckin' statue of Julius Erving in front of the Spectrum, and he was MVP once, won a championship once, but he didn't play his whole career in this town and he wasn't even the best player the Sixers had, not when there was Wilt Chamberlain. Where's Wilt's statue?"

Schmitty worried about his own legacy; his career had been so manic-depressive, he feared for his final place of unrest in the city's hippocampus. Schmitty always worried about something. To those who came so close to loving him, it was his fatal flaw. Julius Erving was pure joy and the fans couldn't wait to build him a monument. Wilt had been castigated as enigmatic, selfish, moody, sybaritic, freak-ish, and too big for his britches.

Schmidt feared the Wilt Factor. He too had been a handful.

But here, at the third base entrance of the new ballpark, is a larger-than-life version of the Greatest Third Baseman of All Time. Ten feet tall and swinging for the fences, hips twisted 90 degrees, right foot on tippy-toes, perfect balance, his metallic eyes following a phantom ball into a phantom upper deck. His lips are sealed. His expression all squint and concentration. No hint of celebration. No cheering. No booing. Arcadia.

But the red is missing, the red of the pinstripes, of the number 20 on his back, the belt, the sleeves. This thick statue is monochromatic, hollow, with no red in the great curls that jut from beneath the red helmet, no red Velcro on his batting gloves, no red stripe around the bat. He always had a red aura. Choleric.

On the base of the sculpture, it reads, "Phillies Hall of Fame Third Baseman. 1972–1989," as if he had lived for those seventeen years and perished. After his playing days, he wanted to be a manager. He knows an awful lot of baseball. But the Greatest Third Baseman of

All Time was never comfortable with baseball bosses, and vice versa.

Baseball likes simplicity, good or bad, win or lose, and Schmidt was All-Star ambiguity. He could be goat and hero at the same time, smash a ball against the center field wall and sulk into second base. Boo. He neither found release nor offered it. Somehow, this immortal player always reminded us of our own mortality. Boo. Athletes are supposed to sublimate anxieties when under fire; block them or dump them or surmount them or spit in their faces. Mike Schmidt wore them on his uniform like a general's four stars. He emanated conflict. Boo. He blamed the fans for bullying him, he praised the fans for pushing him. Boo. They got him down, they stirred him up. A great player, like a great artist, gives you back more than you bring to him. Mike Schmidt demanded too much. He was exhausting. Boooooooo.

I can't help but remember the story he told as I sit here and stare at this enormous bronzed action figure.

"It's the classic game of my career," he started. "It was 1983, when we had Rose, Morgan, Perez. We were home against Montreal, and I struck out four times on twelve pitches—three, three, three, three. Probably the only time in the history of the sport. It was a tie game, 1–1. Every time I came up, the fans cheered. They were standing, clapping, because they knew I was the guy who could win the game with one swing. I had done it before, and they anticipated it, a home run to win the game. After every strikeout, they booed me all the way back to the dugout. Viciously. I turned to Tony Perez and said, 'Tony, I gotta get out of this game. I gotta retire. I gotta quit. I can't take it anymore. There is no reason to put myself through this kind of worry and frustration.' Thirty-three thousand people were booing me. And this is my home ballpark. No one can imagine what that's like. You feel the hatred. If any of them had a weapon, I'd be dead.

"The fifth time up, bottom of the tenth, Jeff Reardon on the mound, two outs, and it's mighty hard to walk up there to home plate. You want to hide in a hole, bury yourself. No matter that I had three-hundred-some home runs and a couple MVPs under my belt, a world championship ring, none of that mattered when I walked up there. If I had a gun, I might have shot myself.

"I hit a home run. We win the game 2–1. I run around the bases, run across home plate, right up the runway, right into the clubhouse, grab my car keys, right out to the car, and drive home without saying a word to anyone, feeling total hate for the baseball, total hate for the Philadelphia fan, hate for everything. Why does any human being have to go through what I just went through? Nothing could have been worse than what was going on in my life at that moment.

"The next day, it was all over. The game was in the books. The only one who remembers is me."

And me. I think of that game whenever I see a young player, a snot-nose kid, come up in the bottom of the ninth with a chance to win it all, dig in his heels, take a few deep breaths to exhale the memories of Wiffle Ball in the backyard with a stern dad and slumps in the pony league in some podunk town, a kid from outside Des Moines or a Dominican shantytown, take a few rehearsal cuts, as if he could forget how to swing, and finally step into the batter's box, excited to have the chance to do what he and a million kids just like him have dreamed about doing, what Mike Schmidt did that night in the tenth inning.

Sign with the Kansas City Royals, kid. Philly can be cruel.

Broad Street ends when you see the whites of the eyes of the guard at the Navy Yard. It hasn't been a functioning Navy yard for the last decade, not because of any change in the nature of man, only the nature of his wars. But "Navy Yard" is a good name and refuses to be jettisoned after two hundred years of service. A gated community now, nearly a thousand acres of land where the Delaware and Schuylkill rivers converge, it awaits occupants, commercial and residential, pioneers of the next Philly neighborhood. The guard politely whisks me through without a single question.

It's cross between a lush state college campus and a suburban office park in Oregon, with bucolic green fields for Frisbee tossing and the classic brick buildings of libraries and deans' residences. Of course, there is the river in the background, and the ships, mothballed cruisers and destroyers sitting on the water like prodigious prehistoric birds, an aircraft carrier three football fields long and twenty stories high. There are five graving docks where a few new ships will be built each year, tankers and container vessels, nothing suited for battle, for an invasion of Iran. They are owned by Kvaerner, Europe's largest commercial shipbuilder, which ponied up a couple hundred million dollars.

When low-flying planes pass overhead, it's easy to imagine yourself in a scene from a black and white World War II movie. And more planes fly to and from the nearby Philadelphia International Airport than cars drive on the ground. This would be a fine place to give your kids driving lessons, wide streets and empty. Or teach them how to drive a golf ball. Five golf courses could fit comfortably in this one-thousand-acre annex. For a comparison, Disneyland is 160 acres. Googleplex, the world headquarters of Google, accumulator of all the knowledge in the world, takes up thirty acres in the Silicon Valley.

Among the seventy businesses operating here, the most impressive is Urban Outfitters, the clothing and accessory company that renovated four buildings (#7, #10, #15, and #543) and moved all 625 employees to the Navy Yard. What was the lure?

"We have a number of people who wanted to bring their dogs to work," said Richard Hayne, president of U.O. "So when we first started looking at high-rise buildings downtown, even if dogs were allowed, which they weren't, I thought, 'Where would they walk them?'"

In the world's largest off-leash unpoliced dog park. And if the pets like to swim, this is doggy paradise. But since most businesses don't give a poop about their employees' dogs, the Navy Yard remains a hard sell, even with tax incentives. You need a car to get here, a Vespa to get around. And where would you go? There are a couple cafeterias, but you won't find a pharmacy or a stationery store or a place to fix your handbag during lunch break. A pet supply store would do well.

The master planners are throwing around large numbers, billions of dollars and tens of thousands of jobs. There has been talk of a movie studio, a health spa, a casino, a mall, million-dollar mansions, affordable housing, high-rise condos, a research park, a swanky marina district, restaurants and hotels for the future ocean liner disembarkers. And then there's the Olympics. That's right, the Summer Olympiad of 2016. In South Philadelphia. Home of Frankie Avalon and Skinny Joey Merlino, the wild mob boss with weaknesses for casinos, softball, the spotlight, and armored trucks.

The sports venues are close by, the eateries and hotels of Center City are a few miles due north, the rivers make security easier, and the Navy Yard already resembles an Olympic Village of sorts. Extend the Broad Street subway and you have rapid transportation. Philadelphia has formed a committee and is hawking the idea big-time. Damn. Folks sure are feeling good about themselves around here. Going up against LA and San Fran and Chicago, and then the world. All that's missing is solid support from the good citizens of the potential host city.

How many Philadelphians would appreciate all the money and fuss spent to gussy up the old Navy Yard for foreigners and media-heads, for endless inconveniences and difficulties getting to Phillies games? Philadelphians are not in the habit of rolling out the red carpet. In addition to the traditional five interlocking circles, the International Olympic Committee would have to plaster the town with signs imploring No Battery Throwing, No Booing Gold Medalists, No Cheering Major Injuries, No Drinking After the Seventh Event of the Decathlon. One can see the *Action News* helicopter covering the midnight storming of the Olympic Village by some downtown toughs trying to hook up with the Italian women's volleyball team.

"Yo, Antny, didja see the spikes on da server?"

"Drop the baseball bats and put your hands up in the air."

In one spectacular public relations gymnastic vault, Philadelphia could catapult itself from ex–national joke to global laughingstock.

Sitting by the river, trying not to make too much sense of the last twenty-four hours, just watching dark ripples going nowhere, somewhere, you hope they drop the Olympic torch. Let the people enjoy the rejuvenated esprit de corps in Philly fashion.

Too sophisticated, not to say jaded, to fall for all the post-9/11 hype, Philadelphians will handle this chrysalis of affirmation with their usual disdain. What's a *National Geographic Traveler* anyway? No one watches PBS shows about urban renewal. Eden this! A compliment is nice, but scrappy underdogs take that bone home and bury it in the backyard. Philadelphians know the opposite of a last-minute reprieve is a last-second disaster. Philadelphians know a lot of families were having the best day of their lives on beautiful beaches when that Asian tsunami hit that day after Christmas.

The river rolls by, charcoal gray. Images of the Leni Lenape come to mind, paddling their dugout canoes, fishing these same waters, hunting on this very spot, as they had for thousands of years before the Europeans arrived with their charms and diseases.

Sentimentality is for squares, but you can't repress the past, can't stop Penn and Franklin from floating to the surface of your unconscious and giving you a wink. If the Quakers gave Philadelphians whatever tolerance they possess, Ben Franklin gave them nearly everything else—the first library, first hospital, first fire company, first insurance company, first bifocals, and first American Declaration of Independence. Did I mention the Franklin stove? He may have been, all at the same time, the country's best writer, inventor, scientist, diplomat, business strategist, and all-around thinker. Did I mention electricity? He didn't even want a patent on or a profit from his lightning rod. He bequeathed his adopted city literacy, humor, a journalistic tradition, a scientific curiosity, a taste for lager, for the ladies, and French connections. He could dance and cook and he could sing his babies to sleep.

He took daily walks, walked the same Broad Street I just walked, visited with tailors and Army recruiters and vendors and vagrants. A harmonious multitude, he called it. Bartenders with the gift of gab and boxers with a punching bag for a future. How he would have loved to walk the thirteen miles of 14th Street and meet Philadelphians from Guyana and China, first-generation cooks and fifth-generation firemen, laborers with accents from five thousand miles away and from 5th and Shunk.

He would embrace the Internet (if he didn't invent it) and buy shares in Comcast (if he didn't own it) and he would surely bound around town with a souped-up phone with Bluetooth technology and a megapixel camera, GPS capability, EVDO, and . . . my cell phone is ringing.

"Where are you now?"

"At the river," I say.

"Don't jump," says my brother.

"Not funny," I say.

"You sound down."

"Not down, not up. Reflective."

"So, did you find what you were looking for?"

"What was I looking for?"

"I don't know. Some kind of closure."

"For starters, I don't believe in closures."

"Can I ask you a question without you getting mad?"

"Sure."

"Are you mad at me?"

"For what?"

"For staying home with Mom when you got sent away to school?"

"Where did that come from?"

"Are you?"

"I don't think so."

"Then what are you so mad about?"

"That I couldn't stay home too."

"That was a long time ago, brother," he says.

"There's no such thing as time," I say.

"Tell that to Verizon when I get my bill."

"Remember *Be Here Now* by Ram Dass?"

"Like it was yesterday," he says.

"I think I understand what now is now."

"I don't have much time. Tell me fast."

"It's not that the past fills you with regret and the future makes you nervous. It's that there is no past or future."

"That's what my girlfriend told me ten minutes ago," he says.

"Really?"

"She said we have no future and she's forgotten our past."

"I'm being serious. It's not that they don't exist, it's just that they're all happening all the time—in something called 'now.' Like three angels dancing on the head of a pin, hand in hand, intertwined and inseparable."

"Speaking of angels, you going to the cemetery before you leave?"

"Should I?"

"I would if I were in Philly."

"Easy for you to say. You've been in California for twenty years."

"Twenty-five years, brother. Time flies."

"How come it's always the most mistreated child who stays close to home and takes care of the parents?" I ask.

"I don't know. That's next semester."

"Remember when I introduced you to the rabbi at the cemetery?"

"I was with Lala and Ben," he says.

"You had your blind dog in one hand and your son in the other?"

"Lala was a good dog."

"Do you remember what you said to the rebbe?"

"Hello, this is my bitch and this is my bastard."

"That's right."

"Wait a minute. I have another call," he says.

"I'll hold . . . mmm . . . mmm . . . mmm . . ."

"Speaking of bitches . . ."

"I thought you two were finished."

"That was the plan."

"Things never work out the way . . ."

Click.

POSTAMBLE

BACK in New York, I sit down to dinner with my wife, the cool, cool kitty from New York City. She asks about walking Broad Street. After a bottle of zinfandel, I want to tell her how nice it is to be home, to be with her, to be spending my life with her, but I clam up.

"What's the matter?" she asks.

"Tired is all," I say.

I am afraid to tell her that I am afraid to tell her what I want to tell her. We have been married a long time and she can read me like a Gypsy. She puts down her wineglass and leans forward.

"Say it," she whispers. "It's okay. You're not in Philadelphia anymore."

She looks beautiful. I look away, through a window. I see the moon. It looks like green cheese.

"That's what you think," I say.